The Unseen Battlefield: Tales of Experimentation and Ingenuity in World War II

The Untold Story of Secret Weapons, Experimental Tanks, Guided Missiles, and Covert Tactics That Transformed World War II—How Innovation, Battlefield Engineering, and Military Strategy Shaped Modern Warfare

Nathaniel Royce

Copyright © 2025 Nathaniel Royce

Disclaimer

This book is a work of historical analysis and documentation. While every effort has been made to ensure the accuracy of the information presented, the author and publisher make no representations or warranties regarding the completeness, reliability, or suitability of the content for any specific purpose.

The content is based on historical sources, declassified military documents, personal testimonies, and secondary research. However, interpretations of historical events may vary among historians and military experts. The author has made every effort to present the material in an accurate and balanced manner, but readers are encouraged to conduct further research to form their own conclusions.

This book is not intended as a definitive military guide, nor does it advocate for war, violence, or political ideologies. Its purpose is to explore the innovative strategies, technological advancements, and battlefield ingenuity that emerged during World War II, providing readers with a deeper understanding of military history and its impact on modern warfare.

Any opinions expressed are those of the author and do not necessarily reflect the views of any military institution, government, or organization. The author and publisher disclaim any liability for decisions made based on the information provided in this book.

For further historical research, readers are encouraged to consult primary sources, government archives, and academic works on the subject.

Contents

• • •

Chapter 1:
Introduction – The
Unconventional
Battlefield

When I think back on those harrowing days of
World War II, I'm struck by how the chaos of battle

forced ordinary people to tap into extraordinary creativity. It wasn't just about armies clashing—it was a time when necessity became a spark for innovation, when every scrap of metal and every discarded tool had the potential to be reborn into something that could make a difference.

I remember reading a diary entry from a soldier in autumn 1943 that perfectly captures the spirit of that era:

> "Today, I witnessed a sight that defies logic and stokes the embers of both fear and admiration. A makeshift armored vehicle, cobbled together from the wreckage of our past and the fervor of our present, rumbled past the shattered remnants of what once was home. Its engine roared like a wounded beast, yet in that discordant symphony, I heard the resolute heartbeat of survival."

In that moment, the battlefield wasn't just a place of destruction—it was a vast, unpredictable workshop where engineers and mechanics, often working under dire circumstances, transformed desperation into hope. Factories that once hummed with routine production were suddenly filled with the clatter of improvisation, as ingenious minds repurposed every spare piece into a tool of survival.

I'm drawn to this story because it's a story of human resilience. Amidst the roar of engines, the clang of metal, and the ever-present tension of uncertainty, there was also a raw, human connection. People weren't merely surviving; they were creating, adapting, and fighting back with every bit of ingenuity they could muster. It's the kind of innovation that wasn't born in a lab under controlled conditions, but in the heat of battle, where every invention carried a mix of hope and heartbreak.

Imagine standing in a dimly lit workshop, the air thick with the smell of oil and burning metal. There, an engineer works feverishly by candlelight, sketching out designs on scraps of paper, his hands trembling not from fear but from the sheer intensity of determination. Each improvised contraption wasn't just a machine—it was a testament to the human spirit, a declaration that even in our darkest hours, creativity can shine through.

Another diary entry, from the bitter winter of 1944, comes to mind:

> "I found myself in the workshop of a defiant soul—a man who believed that every shattered gear and twisted wire held the promise of salvation. As he toiled under the faint glow of a makeshift lamp, his hands danced over

the cold metal, breathing life into what many deemed useless. In that moment, I realized that our war was not just fought on the battlefield, but in the hearts and minds of those who refused to surrender to fate."

This isn't just a tale of machines and tactics—it's a story of people, their hopes, their fears, and their relentless will to survive. It's about the creativity that emerges when you're backed into a corner and the rules of ordinary life no longer apply. On this unconventional battlefield, every improvised weapon and every innovative design tells a personal story, echoing the bravery and the resourcefulness of its maker.

So, as we begin this journey together, let's step into a world where every scrap, every clank of metal, and every flash of ingenuity was a lifeline. Welcome to the unconventional battlefield—a place where war was fought not only with might and metal, but with the unyielding human spirit, daring to reimagine the very essence of conflict.

Chapter 2: Global Pressures – The Climate of Innovation

When the world stood on the precipice of collapse, the relentless pressures of global conflict reshaped not only nations but the very essence of human ingenuity. In the tumultuous years of World War II, every nation was forced into a crucible where conventional military might was rendered insufficient by unprecedented resource shortages and unyielding geopolitical rivalries. In this environment, scarcity and conflict were not merely obstacles—they were the raw materials from which innovation was forged.

In cities across Europe and America, familiar production lines ground to a halt as factories were retooled overnight. Industrial complexes that once churned out consumer goods transformed into chaotic hubs of rapid prototyping and emergency manufacturing. Steel, rubber, and fuel—all once abundant—became precious commodities, prompting military leaders and engineers to innovate with every discarded bolt and scrap of metal they could salvage. The scarcity of these vital materials meant that every decision in the war effort was colored by a sense of urgency, where even the smallest component could tip the scales between defeat and survival.

I remember reading a diary entry from a British military strategist during the bitter winter of 1940. In the cold, dim light of his underground command center, he recorded:

> "Tonight, as I pore over hastily drawn blueprints by the flicker of a single candle, the weight of our shortages presses down on us like a physical force. We are fighting on two fronts— the visible enemy outside and an invisible war waged against time,

scarcity, and our own limitations. Yet
even in this oppressive darkness, I
glimpse sparks of genius, sketches that
promise to reshape our future."

This entry captures the dual battle fought by those
at the heart of the war. Beyond the visible carnage
on battlefields, there was an internal struggle—a
battle of wills against the relentless depletion of
resources. In London, where the constant threat of
aerial bombardment was compounded by the daily
reality of rationing, every strategic decision was
made with the stark understanding that there was
no margin for error. Every lost shipment of raw
materials or delayed production run was a blow not
just to military capability, but to national morale.

In the war-torn streets of Paris and the industrial
corridors of American cities, the spirit of innovation
was a direct response to these challenges. In a
cramped, bomb-damaged workshop beneath the
ruins of Paris, a young engineer recorded his
determination:

"By the meager light of a salvaged
bulb, I've learned to see beauty in
broken things. Each piece of scrap
metal tells a story—of battles fought, of
lives upended. And tonight, I will turn
these remnants into something that
might just save us tomorrow."

Across the vast expanses of the Soviet Union, where brutal winters compounded the hardships of war, communities clung to this same belief. In a small village in the snowbound outskirts of Moscow, resourcefulness was not a luxury but a daily necessity. Families repurposed farm tools into makeshift weapons, and entire neighborhoods pooled their limited supplies of metal and fuel to support local workshops. In these isolated outposts, ingenuity was a quiet, defiant rebellion against the overwhelming odds, a tangible reminder that nothing was ever truly wasted.

The geopolitical rivalries of the era added yet another layer of pressure. The Axis and Allied powers were engaged in a high-stakes contest that transcended mere territorial disputes. It was a battle of ideologies, where the failure to innovate could mean not only military defeat but the collapse of an entire way of life. In boardrooms and war rooms, debates raged over alternative materials and novel production methods. Military planners shifted their focus from the accumulation of traditional firepower to the creative reimagining of every available resource. This was not the war of muscle and might alone—it was the war of ideas, where every shortage was met with a bold new approach.

One vivid account from an American factory manager illustrates the transformative power of these pressures. Amid the relentless hum of assembly lines that had once produced automobiles, workers now found themselves reconfiguring machines to churn out parts for new, experimental weaponry. In a candid letter home, he wrote:

> "Every day, I watch men and women reinventing what we thought was unchangeable. With every piece of metal we repurpose, there's a spark of hope that we might just outsmart the enemy. It's as if the very act of creation has become our weapon."

This profound sense of urgency gave rise to a culture where failure was not an option. Innovations were developed on tight deadlines, often under conditions that would have been deemed impossible in peacetime. In the laboratories of occupied Europe, engineers worked feverishly, drawing on every ounce of creativity to turn scarcity into an asset. They experimented with makeshift alloys, improvised circuitry, and repurposed machinery, transforming what was available into something radically new. Every breakthrough was celebrated not merely as a technical achievement but as a lifeline—a tangible proof that ingenuity could flourish even amidst chaos.

The broader geopolitical landscape underscored the importance of these innovations. In strategic briefings held in war rooms across continents, commanders debated how the loss of one critical resource might necessitate a complete overhaul of military strategy. In these high-pressure meetings, the conversation was as much about economics and logistics as it was about weaponry and tactics. Leaders from opposing sides were forced to acknowledge that the scarcity of resources was a universal challenge—a challenge that, in many ways, leveled the playing field and forced even the most powerful nations to innovate.

Yet, amid all this strategic maneuvering and industrial adaptation, the human element remained at the forefront. The anxiety that pervaded the global stage was not an abstract concept—it was a lived reality for millions. Families endured rationed meals, children went to bed hungry, and communities lived in constant fear of the next air raid or missile strike. And yet, in the midst of such despair, there was a profound and unwavering determination to not only survive but to create. The very act of innovation became a symbol of resistance, a quiet yet powerful declaration that even in the worst of times, humanity would not surrender its capacity to dream, to build, and to overcome.

In one particularly moving account from a Soviet engineer, the sense of purpose was palpable:

> "In the silence of the night, with the
> bitter cold seeping into our bones, we

gathered around a creaking workbench. There was no time for lamenting the shortages; we had only one option—to build something out of nothing. Each invention was a small victory against the encroaching darkness, a reminder that even in the harshest winter, there is a warmth born of human resolve."

This climate of unparalleled pressure did more than spur technological breakthroughs—it redefined the very nature of warfare. Every innovation was a direct response to a specific, often desperate, need. The creative solutions that emerged during these years set in motion a series of changes that would eventually influence military strategies for decades to come. The war was no longer fought solely on the battleground; it was also waged in the workshops, laboratories, and hidden basements where ordinary people transformed dire scarcity into extraordinary ingenuity.

Reflecting on this era, one can see that the innovations born of necessity during World War II were as much about human survival as they were about technological advancement. They were a testament to the idea that even when the odds are overwhelmingly against us, the human spirit can find ways to turn adversity into advantage. Every shortage, every resource constraint, became not just a limitation but a powerful incentive to innovate—a legacy that reminds us that progress is often forged in the fires of crisis.

This chapter has explored the multifaceted pressures that defined an era. From the cramped, candlelit workshops in bombed-out cities to the expansive, hurried production floors of American factories, we witness a world in which every challenge demanded a radical new approach. It is in this pressure-cooker environment that the seeds of modern warfare were sown—a legacy of creativity and resilience that continues to resonate today.

The narrative of global pressures and resource scarcity is not simply a chronicle of hardship. It is a story of hope, of innovation, and of the relentless drive to adapt in the face of overwhelming odds. As we continue our journey through this book, we carry forward the lessons learned in this crucible of conflict—lessons that remind us how the interplay of necessity and creativity can redefine what is possible, even in the darkest times.

Chapter 3: Necessity as Inspiration – Invention Under Fire

In the raging inferno of World War II, amid the relentless thunder of artillery and the ever-looming shadow of death, necessity emerged as the single most potent driver of human innovation. In these extraordinary times, survival depended not on conventional wisdom or well-practiced routines, but on the raw, unbridled power of creativity under pressure. With every passing day, as the chaos of war encroached upon every facet of life, engineers, mechanics, and soldiers alike were forced to abandon routine and embrace a frantic, yet ingenious, spirit of experimentation.

A Crucible of Urgency and Imagination

Under the constant barrage of enemy fire and the oppressive reality of dwindling supplies, traditional modes of production and military strategy were rendered obsolete. The harsh conditions of wartime—bombed-out factories, scarcity of raw materials, and the ever-present specter of defeat—created an environment where every discarded scrap of metal and every broken tool held the promise of a new beginning. It was a time when innovation wasn't a luxury; it was a desperate imperative.

In the chaos of a makeshift workshop hidden beneath the rubble of a once-thriving European city, engineers were compelled to reimagine the very tools of warfare. Walls that had once supported the normal cadence of life now echoed with the clamor of improvised machinery. Against the backdrop of constant danger, every invention was rushed from concept to reality with a speed that defied the usual careful deliberation of peacetime research and development.

In one such hidden workshop, illuminated only by the sporadic light of a salvaged lantern, a young engineer named René labored over a contraption built from nothing more than scavenged automobile parts and remnants of military hardware. His journal, written in spidery, trembling script, reads:

> "Every spark from my soldering iron feels like a defiant shout against the encroaching darkness. With each weld, I'm not just fusing metal; I'm fusing hope with despair, turning our inevitable loss into a tangible chance to fight back. The machine before me might be crude, but it carries with it the desperate promise of survival."

René's words capture the essence of the era—a time when each improvised solution was as much a personal triumph as it was a tactical necessity. In these underground sanctuaries of innovation, the boundaries between survival and invention blurred. The very act of building something new was an act of rebellion against the overwhelming odds and a steadfast declaration that the human spirit could never be fully extinguished.

The Soldier as an Accidental Inventor

On the frontlines, the spirit of rapid experimentation was equally alive. The battlefield itself became a vast, unpredictable laboratory where soldiers, often armed with nothing more than their instinct and a handful of salvaged parts, transformed desperation into ingenuity. Sergeant James "Jim" O'Connell, a hardened veteran of several brutal engagements, once recounted his experience during a prolonged siege when ammunition ran dangerously low.

With enemy fire pounding their positions and traditional supply lines severed, Jim and his comrades resorted to a form of improvised engineering that defied the rigid doctrines of military logistics. In a rare moment of quiet amidst the chaos, he wrote in a letter home:

> "We were trapped between relentless enemy fire and our own failing supplies. With no official orders or manuals to guide us, we began repurposing parts of our broken-down artillery to craft munitions by hand. It wasn't about perfection—it was about survival. Every makeshift round we produced carried the weight of our desperation and the stubborn will to keep fighting."

For Jim, the battlefield was more than a place of mortal peril—it was a crucible that transformed ordinary soldiers into resourceful inventors. Each improvised device, each quick fix under fire, was a testament to the relentless human drive to adapt when all conventional options were stripped away. The ingenuity borne out of these extreme conditions was not merely tactical; it was deeply personal—a raw expression of defiance against a system that had forsaken them.

The Workshop of War: A Symphony of Desperation and Creativity

The rapid pace of wartime experimentation was a phenomenon that spanned continents. In a clandestine laboratory hidden beneath a ruined church in Italy, a team of engineers and mechanics huddled around a rickety workbench, pooling their collective expertise to transform salvaged components into a new type of anti-tank weapon. The room was thick with the smell of oil and burning metal, the air vibrating with the constant clatter of hurried assembly. One veteran mechanic, Marco, later recalled the experience with a mixture of humor and reverence:

> "There we were, a bunch of misfits in a makeshift lab, turning what looked like junk into something that could actually stop a tank. We laughed, we cursed, and we worked as if our lives

depended on every screw we tightened. In those frantic hours, every failure was a lesson, and every success—even a small one—felt like we'd turned the tide of fate itself."

Marco's account speaks to the collective spirit of innovation that pervaded these shadowy corners of wartime industry. Every tool assembled in such workshops was an embodiment of hope, a small beacon in the darkness that declared, "We will not go quietly into the night." In these moments of extreme crisis, the boundaries of science and survival merged, creating a landscape where every idea, no matter how rough or unpolished, could become a crucial instrument of defense.

Intimacy in Innovation: Lives Entwined with Their Creations

The intertwining of life and invention during wartime was a phenomenon marked by raw emotion and intimate personal sacrifice. Every machine crafted in the heat of battle carried with it the fingerprints, sweat, and sometimes even the tears of its creator. For many, the act of innovating was as much about preserving a piece of their identity as it was about constructing a weapon.

In a cramped, smoke-filled room in a French resistance safe house, a resourceful engineer named Lucie documented her daily struggles against both the enemy and the relentless march of time. Her diary entry, penned in careful yet hurried handwriting, reveals the intimate relationship between her work and her very survival:

> "Every night, as I sit at my workbench surrounded by the remnants of what once was a life of normalcy, I rebuild not just machines, but my own hope. Each piece of metal that I mend, each circuit that I rewire, feels like a step toward reclaiming a future stolen by war. I am not just crafting a tool—I am crafting a new way of living, a way of fighting back against the despair that threatens to overwhelm us."

Lucie's reflections remind us that behind every innovative contraption lay a human story—a narrative woven with threads of fear, determination, and the unwavering belief that even in the midst of chaos, beauty and purpose could be found. The engineers, mechanics, and soldiers of this era were not merely inventors; they were poets of survival, crafting lines of hope in the language of metal and fire.

The Ripple Effect of Desperation

The innovations born from these extreme conditions did more than just offer a temporary reprieve from the immediate dangers of war—they planted the seeds for a future where necessity would continue to be a driving force in technological progress. The rapid experimentation seen on battlefields and in hidden workshops laid the groundwork for post-war advancements in engineering, medicine, and even computing. The lessons learned in those desperate hours have echoed through the decades, reminding us that some of the greatest breakthroughs are often conceived in the crucible of crisis.

As we reflect on the turbulent days when invention was a matter of life and death, it becomes clear that the legacy of wartime innovation is not solely about the machines that roared across battlefields. It is about the indomitable human spirit that refused to surrender, the collective ingenuity that turned tragedy into triumph, and the intimate bonds forged between individuals and the creations that carried their hopes into the future.

In this chapter, the story of necessity transforming into inspiration is told not only through blueprints and mechanical parts but through the intimate, often painful, reflections of those who lived it. From the desperate scribbles of a young engineer in a bombed-out city to the improvised brilliance of soldiers on the frontlines, the narrative of innovation under fire is as rich and complex as the human experience itself. Each invention, however makeshift, was a declaration that even when the world seemed poised to crumble, there remained an unyielding belief in the power of creativity to rebuild and renew.

Thus, amid the fire and fury of war, as machines were born from the embers of devastation and dreams were soldered together in the darkest hours, a powerful truth emerged: in the crucible of necessity, the human spirit can ignite a flame of innovation so fierce that it lights the way forward, even through the deepest shadows of despair.

Chapter 4: Armored Oddities – The Rise of Experimental Tanks

In the dark, tumultuous days of World War II, the battlefield was not only defined by the thunder of artillery or the crackle of radio static—it was also sculpted by the roar of engines and the clashing of metal. As the war raged on, conventional armored vehicles were found wanting in a conflict that demanded unprecedented innovation. Out of this crucible of necessity and daring experimentation emerged a host of unconventional tanks and armored vehicles—machines as audacious in design as they were vital on the battlefield.

Forging the Unconventional

Engineers and military strategists faced an impossible task: to design vehicles that could withstand the relentless barrage of modern warfare while outsmarting an enemy that adapted just as quickly. Traditional tank designs, with their predictable silhouettes and proven armaments, were suddenly seen as relics of a bygone era. In secret workshops and bombed-out factories, teams of inventors began to sketch blueprints that defied convention.

One such blueprint—scribbled on weathered paper by a visionary engineer known only by his first name, "Erik"—revealed an experimental tank prototype dubbed the "Iron Chimera." Unlike the bulky, box-like forms of standard tanks, the Iron Chimera featured a streamlined chassis with an overhanging glacis plate designed to deflect incoming shells. Its turret, offset to one side, was an audacious departure from symmetry, intended to maximize the firing arc while minimizing the vehicle's frontal profile. Detailed schematics showed angled armor plating, reinforced joints, and an innovative suspension system that promised a smoother ride over the uneven, war-torn terrain.

The technical blueprints, marked with meticulous notations—"reinforce here for recoil management," "optimize track tension"—were as much works of art as they were engineering guides. They depicted cross-sectional views of the engine compartment, where a custom-built V12 diesel roared to life, channeling power through a labyrinthine system of gears and transmissions. Every line on the blueprint spoke to a desperate need for speed, agility, and survivability in a battlefield that was as unforgiving as it was unpredictable.

The Symphony of Steel and Fire

In the midst of these creative fermentations, the soundscape of war provided both inspiration and a constant reminder of what was at stake. The factory floors became stages for a relentless symphony of clanging metal, hissing steam, and the deep, thunderous roar of engines coming to life. In one particularly memorable moment, I recall standing in a cavernous hangar where a prototype tank was undergoing its first shakedown test. The vehicle's engine erupted in a raw, guttural roar that echoed off the concrete walls, mingling with the clatter of heavy chains and the metallic clang of rivets being driven into armored plates.

The vibrations of the engine seemed to carry with them the very heartbeat of the machine—a pulse born of ingenuity and desperation. Observers described the experience as standing in the presence of a living, breathing beast; one that had been assembled piece by piece from the remnants of a shattered world. Every rev of the engine and every scrape of metal against metal was a testament to the audacity of its creators, who had dared to challenge the conventions of warfare with designs that bordered on the fantastical.

Innovation Born from Necessity

The rise of experimental tanks was not merely an exercise in engineering bravado—it was a matter of survival. Traditional armored vehicles, with their predictable armor schemes and fixed armaments, were increasingly vulnerable to the evolving tactics of enemy forces. The advent of new anti-tank weapons, coupled with the unpredictability of modern warfare, demanded a radical rethinking of what a tank could be.

In response, engineers developed vehicles with modular designs that could be rapidly reconfigured in the field. One experimental model featured interchangeable turret systems, allowing soldiers to adapt the vehicle's armament depending on the tactical situation. Blueprints for this design revealed a clever system of quick-release fittings and integrated wiring harnesses, enabling a nearly seamless transition from a high-caliber cannon to a rapid-fire machine gun turret. The technical documents noted, "Field adaptability is paramount—must support reconfiguration in under 15 minutes."

Another innovative design attempted to solve the problem of limited mobility on rough, debris-strewn battlefields. Known colloquially as the "Crawler," this experimental vehicle featured an extended track system and an advanced suspension mechanism that spread the vehicle's weight over a larger surface area. The result was a machine capable of traversing terrain that would have immobilized even the most robust conventional tank. The blueprint of the Crawler illustrated a network of interconnected hydraulic dampers and adjustable tensioners, all designed to ensure that the vehicle maintained traction, even in the thick mud and rubble of a devastated urban landscape.

Blueprints of Bold Ambition

The technical blueprints that emerged during this period were filled with annotations and revisions—a visual diary of the iterative process that defined wartime innovation. Every sketch bore the fingerprints of its creator, whether it was the meticulous measurements along the edges of an

● ● ●

armored plate or the hurried notes scribbled in the margins about improving engine performance. These documents not only served as guides for assembly but also as historical records of an era when necessity drove men and women to the very limits of their creative potential.

Consider, for example, the schematic of a prototype turret mounting system that appeared in several of the experimental designs. The drawing depicted a radically new approach: instead of a static, fixed turret, the system allowed for a slight degree of lateral movement. This innovation was intended to absorb the recoil of powerful armaments, thereby reducing the strain on the vehicle's chassis. Diagrams showed detailed measurements of shock-absorbing materials, pivot points, and reinforced mounting brackets. These technical notes, though highly specialized, resonated with the broader narrative of a time when every technical improvement was a potential lifeline on the battlefield.

Tales from the Assembly Line

The stories of these armored oddities are as much about the machines as they are about the people who built them. In a makeshift assembly line in a repurposed factory on the outskirts of Berlin, I once met a veteran welder named Klaus who had dedicated his life to constructing these experimental tanks. With grease-stained overalls and eyes that sparkled with a mix of exhaustion and fierce pride, Klaus recounted the challenges of working with untested designs:

> "Every day was a gamble," Klaus said, his voice rough like the metal he worked with. "We were given blueprints that seemed to change with every new threat. One moment, you're welding a plate that might never see the light of day; the next, it's the difference between life and death on the battlefield. The roar of the engine as you fire up a new prototype—that sound... it gives you hope. It tells you that what we're building isn't just metal and bolts—it's our chance to fight back."

Klaus's words paint a vivid picture of life on the assembly line, where the act of creation was intertwined with the raw emotions of fear, hope, and defiance. The clashing of metal as tanks were assembled was not merely a mechanical process—it was the sound of determination, a relentless drive to transform the dire circumstances of war into a future defined by possibility.

The Impact on Battlefield Tactics

As these experimental tanks began to emerge from the secretive workshops and cluttered assembly lines, their impact on battlefield tactics was profound. Commanders who had grown weary of the predictable vulnerabilities of standard tanks found that these unconventional designs brought new advantages—and new risks. The Iron Chimera, with its angled armor and offset turret, offered improved deflection against incoming shells but also required a novel approach to maneuvering in combat. Meanwhile, vehicles like the Crawler, with their extended track systems, could outflank enemy positions and navigate obstacles that would have halted a conventional tank in its tracks.

The new designs forced military strategists to rethink their assumptions. Battles became a chess match where each experimental machine represented both an opportunity and a gamble—a high-risk, high-reward proposition that could tip the scales of war in an instant. The technical advancements documented in the blueprints were not just academic exercises; they were the foundations upon which new doctrines of armored warfare were built.

A Legacy of Steel and Innovation

In retrospect, the era of experimental tanks and armored oddities stands as one of the most fascinating chapters in the history of military technology. It was a time when the constraints of limited resources and the pressures of imminent threat sparked a wave of creativity that reshaped the very notion of what a tank could be. The technical blueprints, with their intricate details and bold innovations, are a testament to the ingenuity of the engineers who dared to dream beyond the limitations of their era.

The roar of these experimental engines, the clash of metal on metal, and the enduring hum of machinery on the assembly line are echoes of a past where necessity was the mother of invention. These armored oddities, born from the fires of conflict, were more than just vehicles—they were symbols of human resilience, testaments to a spirit that refused to yield even in the face of overwhelming adversity.

As we look back on these remarkable machines, we see not only the technical achievements of a bygone era but also the passion, determination, and sheer audacity of those who built them. Their legacy lives on in the armored vehicles of today—a legacy forged in steel and powered by the relentless drive to innovate under fire.

Chapter 5: Reinventing Firepower – Unconventional Small Arms & Artillery

In the swirling chaos of World War II, where every moment was a struggle for survival, conventional weaponry was quickly outpaced by the evolving demands of battle. The relentless pace of combat demanded rapid adaptation—an evolution where every bullet, every explosion, and every moment of silence between volleys underscored the need to innovate. In this crucible of fire and steel, engineers, soldiers, and mechanics pushed the boundaries of what was possible, transforming standard-issue arms and massive artillery into something altogether more lethal and unpredictable.

The Context of Innovation

As enemy tactics evolved and supply lines buckled under the strain of global conflict, front-line units found themselves at a crossroads. Traditional small arms and artillery, designed during times of peace and predictability, began to falter in the face of a dynamic and brutal new reality. The harsh conditions of modern warfare, compounded by resource shortages and relentless enemy pressure, ignited a spark of creativity among those who dared to dream of a better way to fight.

In makeshift workshops, hidden away in bombed-out basements and repurposed factories, soldiers and engineers worked side by side. Every improvised modification was a direct response to the immediate challenges of the battlefield. In these intense moments of crisis, every alteration was more than a mere technical adjustment—it was a declaration that survival depended on the ability to innovate, to reinvent firepower on the fly.

• • •

Unconventional Modifications to Small Arms

Across the frontlines, even the smallest weapons were not immune to the relentless push for improvement. Soldiers learned that with a few clever modifications, standard-issue rifles and pistols could be transformed into far deadlier tools of war. The ingenuity often came from the most unexpected quarters:

- **Enhanced Barrels and Sights:** Engineers and marksmen worked together to re-bore rifle barrels, increasing their accuracy and effective range. In many cases, salvaged telescopic sights or even repurposed glass from shattered windows were integrated into these designs. The difference was palpable: soldiers spoke of how a once standard rifle now allowed them to engage targets at distances previously thought unattainable.

- **Customized Ammunition:** Field expediency often demanded adjustments to the ammunition itself. Rearranging bullet weights, experimenting with alternative propellants, and even carving out new bullet profiles from old casings were common practices. These modifications improved penetration against enemy armor and enhanced lethality in close-quarter firefights.

- **Ergonomic and Trigger Adjustments:**
  Under fire, every split second counted.
  Soldiers who spent long hours gripping their
  rifles began to fashion custom grips from
  scraps of rubber and wood, while
  mechanics adjusted trigger sensitivities.
  These small tweaks often resulted in a
  dramatic increase in firing speed and
  accuracy—a critical edge when every shot
  could mean the difference between life and
  death.

Private Daniels, a veteran rifleman, recalled one
intense engagement:

> "In the heat of an ambush, our
> standard rifles just weren't cutting it.
> Our sergeant had the foresight to
> cobble together a makeshift scope
> from spare glass and tubing. I
> remember feeling a surge of clarity the
> first time I took aim—the rifle felt alive,
> as if it were perfectly attuned to the
> chaos around us. Every pull of the
> trigger was deliberate, each shot
> echoing with the hope that our
> improvised genius might just save us."

Reimagining Artillery for the New Age of War

While the modifications to small arms were often improvised by individual soldiers, the reinvention of artillery was a more coordinated effort. Artillery, the heavy hitters of the battlefield, had to be rethought from the ground up. The vast, immovable cannons that had once dominated the skies and fields were now subject to rapid transformation:

- **Variable Caliber Systems:** One groundbreaking innovation was the development of artillery systems with variable calibers. These systems allowed a single cannon to switch between high-explosive shells and armor-piercing rounds. Detailed blueprints showed ingenious mechanisms—complex levers and quick-release fittings—that made such rapid transitions possible under fire.
- **Advanced Recoil Absorption:** Traditional artillery suffered from heavy, unwieldy recoil that slowed the rate of fire. Engineers integrated novel recoil absorption systems, combining hydraulic dampers with reinforced mounting brackets. The result was a cannon that could be reloaded and fired at a much faster pace. Captain Marcel, an experienced artillery officer, recalled:

"I still remember the day we retrofitted our 105mm howitzer with a new recoil system fashioned partly from tractor components. The next time it fired, the sound was like thunder rolling over a mountain range. It was as if we had given that old beast a second wind, and it roared with a vengeance we hadn't thought possible."

- **Rapid Field Modifications:** In the face of dwindling supplies, entire artillery batteries were often retrofitted in the field. Crews replaced worn parts with materials scavenged from destroyed vehicles, or even improvised using locally sourced metals. This patchwork of innovation allowed artillery units to continue firing despite chronic shortages, and each modification was meticulously recorded, leaving behind a legacy of technical ingenuity that military historians continue to study.

The Tactile and Auditory Reality of Battle

Innovation on the battlefield was not just about the cold precision of metal and mechanics—it was an experience sensed through every fiber of one's being. The transformation of weapons was a multisensory phenomenon:

- **Tactile Impressions:** The feel of a weapon in hand could change dramatically after modification. Soldiers described the satisfying grip of a retooled rifle, its surface smoothed and balanced to reduce fatigue during long engagements. The vibration of a newly reconfigured howitzer, the firm yet reassuring heft of its controls—each modification was an intimate reminder of the struggle to impose order on chaos.

- **Auditory Impressions:** The sounds of war were a relentless, raw symphony. The staccato bursts of machine gun fire, the deep booms of artillery shells, and the constant clatter of mechanics at work formed a backdrop that was both terrifying and oddly inspiring. Each sound was imbued with the energy of creation—a sonic fingerprint of humanity's refusal to succumb to despair. Sergeant Lisa Moreno, a frontline medic, recalled:

"Even in the midst of a lull between battles, you could hear the metallic clatter as soldiers adjusted their weapons. That sound was more than noise—it was a declaration. It told us that every improvised solution was a promise that we would keep fighting, no matter how dire things got."

Technical Blueprints and Field Adjustments

The evolution of unconventional firepower was meticulously documented in technical blueprints that blended engineering precision with battlefield improvisation. These blueprints were more than just diagrams—they were living records of a rapidly changing art of war:

- **Detailed Schematics:** Every modified firearm and retooled artillery piece was accompanied by hand-drawn schematics. These blueprints detailed changes from the macro to the micro: from the overall dimensions of a new barrel design to the minute adjustments made to trigger sensitivity. Notes in the margins indicated field observations such as, "Improve sight alignment by 0.3 inches" or "Increase bullet velocity with altered powder charge."

- **Iterative Design:** The process was iterative. A prototype might undergo multiple rounds of modifications based on feedback from the frontlines. This feedback loop— engineers receiving firsthand reports from soldiers, adjusting designs accordingly, and then sending revised versions back to the field—became a hallmark of wartime innovation. In one series of diagrams, the progression of a custom rifle modification was outlined step-by-step, with each iteration improving performance under specific combat conditions.

- **Field Manuals:** Eventually, some of these improvised modifications were codified into field manuals. These manuals served as guides for soldiers and mechanics who, in the heat of battle, needed to replicate successful innovations. They were filled with annotated diagrams, clear instructions, and even sketches of the sounds that indicated a weapon was operating optimally—a rare blend of art and science.

Frontline Narratives: Voices from the Fire

The true measure of any innovation lies in the experiences of those who use it. The modifications to small arms and artillery were not theoretical exercises; they were the means by which soldiers turned the tide of battle. Their stories bring to life the human element behind the technical marvels:

- **The Improvised Rifle:** Private Daniels' recollection of a night-time ambush, where his newly modified rifle made all the difference, paints a vivid picture. His words, echoing through the chaos, underscored the deep connection between a soldier and his weapon—a bond forged in the fires of combat.
- **The Reborn Howitzer:** Captain Marcel's account of retrofitting his artillery unit with

an innovative recoil system demonstrates how a single technical breakthrough could invigorate an entire battery. His description of the cannon's roar—like rolling thunder across a frozen landscape—captures both the raw power of the machine and the renewed hope it instilled in his men.

- **The Sound of Innovation:** Sergeant Moreno's memories of the clatter of improvised adjustments, the rapid-fire discussion of last-minute tweaks during lulls in battle, and the visceral impact of each successful modification create a tapestry of sound and sentiment. These auditory memories serve as a constant reminder that every adjustment, no matter how minor, was a step toward survival.

A Legacy Forged in Fire and Steel

The innovative modifications to small arms and artillery during World War II were more than mere adaptations; they were a testament to the indomitable human spirit. In a time when the stakes could not have been higher, every bullet retooled, every cannon retrofitted, and every improvised solution contributed to a legacy that has influenced modern military technology. The creativity born from necessity not only helped win battles but also laid the groundwork for future innovations in weapon design.

The modifications and adaptations documented in those days remind us that the art of war is as much about the human touch as it is about machinery. The hands that reworked a rifle under fire, the minds that recalibrated artillery amidst chaos, and the hearts that beat in unison with the rhythm of survival—all these elements coalesced into a legacy of resilience and ingenuity.

Today, as we study the blueprints, hear the echoes of modified weapons, and read the intimate accounts of soldiers on the frontlines, we are reminded that true innovation often arises in the crucible of adversity. The unconventional modifications to small arms and artillery of World War II remain a poignant symbol of what can be achieved when creativity is born from necessity—a testament to the enduring spirit of those who refused to let the darkness prevail.

Chapter 6: Incendiary Breakthroughs – The Evolution of Flamethrowers

In the searing crucible of World War II, few weapons embodied both terror and transformative innovation like the flamethrower. Born of a desperate need to dislodge entrenched enemy positions, incendiary devices evolved from crude, experimental tools into sophisticated instruments of both psychological and physical warfare. In these pages, we delve deep into the formidable design challenges, the relentless sensory assault of the battlefield, and the human stories behind the evolution of flamethrowers and related incendiary innovations.

Engineering Under Fire

Developing a flamethrower was far more than simply attaching a fuel tank to a nozzle. Engineers confronted a series of daunting technical hurdles that required rapid iteration under the most extreme conditions:

- **Fuel Containment and Delivery:** The volatile nature of fuel meant that early flamethrowers had to securely store flammable liquids under high pressure. Initial designs featured cumbersome, heavy tanks that added unwanted mass and risked catastrophic explosions when struck. Over time, designers experimented with lightweight, heat-resistant alloys and reinforced, modular chassis that not only improved mobility but also enhanced soldier safety.
- **Ignition and Control Systems:** Reliable ignition was critical. Early systems, often

based on rudimentary spark-plug mechanisms or pilot lights, were plagued by misfires and unintended detonations. Iterative improvements led to the development of electronically controlled circuits and redundant safety features that ensured a consistent burst of flame when needed. Detailed schematics from the era reveal intricate wiring diagrams and heat-shielding measures that allowed these systems to function flawlessly amidst the roar of battle.

- **Ergonomic Adaptations:** The weapon had to be operated under extreme stress. Designers rethought every aspect—from the weight distribution of the fuel tanks to the positioning of control levers—to ensure that a soldier, often exhausted and under fire, could aim and deploy the device quickly. Adjustable nozzles, shock-absorbing handles, and intuitive trigger mechanisms became standard as engineers strove to make the flamethrower a natural extension of its operator.

The blueprints of these early models, with annotations scrawled in haste yet precision, read like a diary of trial and error. Each revision was marked by notes such as "increase insulation here" or "reinforce pressure valve," a testament to the relentless pursuit of a design that balanced raw destructive power with the practicalities of field deployment.

The Sensory Onslaught of Incendiary Warfare

On the battlefield, the true measure of a flamethrower was experienced through its overwhelming sensory impact. The transformation of a weapon into a force of nature was not merely mechanical—it was an assault on the senses:

- **Heat That Transcends the Physical:** When a flamethrower discharged, it unleashed a torrent of searing heat that could be felt even at a distance. Soldiers often described the sensation as standing before a wall of fire, where the temperature would suddenly spike, scorching the air and singeing the edges of uniforms. The blast of heat was so intense that it appeared to warp the very fabric of the surrounding landscape, leaving melted remnants in its wake.
- **A Choking Veil of Smoke and Flame:** The discharge of the weapon produced thick, billowing smoke that engulfed the battlefield. Within this suffocating haze, the world transformed into a nightmarish vision— shapes blurred into ghostly forms, and the rapid interplay of light and shadow created

an eerie, otherworldly tableau. Brilliant tongues of flame licked upward, their movements as unpredictable as the enemy they sought to dislodge, while the acrid stench of burning fuel and scorched earth invaded every breath.

- **The Roar and Crackle of Unleashed Destruction:** Auditory memories of the flamethrower are as vivid as the visual and tactile sensations. The initial roar—deep, resonant, and all-consuming—was soon followed by the rapid crackle of fire consuming its fuel. This cacophony was interspersed with the metallic clamor of mechanisms in motion; every adjustment and every spark was a testament to the weapon's intricate engineering and raw power. For soldiers, these sounds were both a harbinger of destruction and a rallying cry in the midst of chaos.

Voices from the Flames

The true power of incendiary devices is best understood through the firsthand accounts of those who wielded them. Their narratives bring to life the profound impact of these weapons on the human psyche and the unfolding of combat:

> "I'll never forget the first time I fired the flamethrower," recalled Corporal

Andre, his voice trembling with a mix of awe and lingering terror. "The moment I squeezed the trigger, a blazing torrent erupted, enveloping everything in a searing embrace. The heat was so intense it felt like an impenetrable wall. In that instant, I saw our enemy's defenses crumble under the force of pure, unbridled fire."

Another poignant recollection came from Sergeant Elena, whose eyes still glisten with the memory of battle:

"Using the flamethrower was like holding a piece of the sun in your hands. The smoke, the overwhelming heat, the deafening roar—it was all so surreal. Every burst of flame not only cleared a path but also etched a mark on your soul. You could feel the intense energy, the raw power of nature harnessed to our will, and it gave you the strength to push forward even in the darkest moments."

These voices, mingling technical precision with raw emotion, capture the dual nature of incendiary innovation. The flamethrower was as much a tool of psychological warfare as it was a mechanical marvel, a symbol of the fierce determination to break enemy lines and, in doing so, to forge a path toward survival.

The Transformative Legacy of Incendiary Innovation

What emerged from the crucible of these design challenges was a weapon that redefined the concept of firepower. The flamethrower and its kin did more than clear bunkers and trenches—they reshaped tactical doctrines and redefined the battlefield experience. Each incremental improvement, documented meticulously in field reports and blueprints, contributed to an evolution that would influence future generations of incendiary munitions and combat systems.

In the relentless heat, billowing smoke, and overwhelming cacophony of battle, the innovations of these incendiary devices resonated beyond their immediate tactical advantages. They became emblems of a period when the desperation of war met the genius of human invention head-on. The legacy of these breakthroughs is visible today in the advanced thermal weapons and defensive systems that continue to bear the imprint of those early, desperate experiments.

In the final analysis, the evolution of flamethrowers stands as a stark reminder of what can be achieved when necessity fuels innovation. In a time when every moment on the battlefield was a struggle against overwhelming odds, the incendiary breakthroughs of World War II lit the way forward—both literally and metaphorically. The heat, the smoke, and the roar of these weapons were not just harbingers of destruction; they were, in their own way, beacons of human resilience and ingenuity, challenging the darkness with the unyielding power of fire.

Chapter 7: Skyward Innovations – Revolutionary Aircraft Design

In the vast expanse above the war-torn battlefields of World War II, the skies became a proving ground for revolutionary ideas. As traditional aircraft designs struggled to keep pace with emerging threats, engineers and pilots embarked on a bold quest to redefine aerial combat. In this chapter, we delve into the experimental fighter planes and bombers that broke new ground, blending meticulous technical schematics with the raw, firsthand experiences of pilots who soared through both the thrill and terror of flight.

Redefining the Skies

Conventional wisdom once dictated that aircraft were simple extensions of ground-based warfare—tools for reconnaissance and strategic bombing. But as enemy defenses grew more sophisticated, the need for rapid maneuverability, improved speed, and stealth became paramount. Visionary engineers began to challenge established doctrines, experimenting with radical designs that defied expectations.

Early experimental prototypes featured features such as:

- **Swept Wings and Delta Configurations:** New wing geometries reduced drag and improved high-speed performance, allowing aircraft to outpace enemy fighters.
- **Enhanced Powerplants:** Custom-engineered engines and turbochargers were integrated into airframes to push the limits of acceleration and altitude performance.
- **Stealth and Countermeasures:** Some designs incorporated early forms of radar-

absorbent materials and innovative exhaust systems to minimize detection.

Detailed technical schematics from classified wartime projects reveal a world of precise engineering: wing cross-sections meticulously measured for optimal lift-to-drag ratios, cockpit layouts reimagined for better pilot visibility and control, and fuselage structures designed to endure extreme aerodynamic stress. Every drawing, annotated with corrections and field notes, was a testament to the relentless pursuit of a new aerial frontier.

The Mechanics Behind the Magic

Blueprints showcased not just the physical dimensions of these experimental machines, but also the integrated systems that allowed for rapid changes in altitude and direction. For instance, one set of schematics revealed an experimental fighter equipped with variable geometry wings—wings that could adjust their sweep angle mid-flight to optimize performance for different combat scenarios. Diagrams detailed the hydraulic systems, electronic controls, and aerodynamic calculations that underpinned this breakthrough.

Another design, a next-generation bomber prototype, featured a streamlined fuselage with a partially pressurized cockpit to help pilots cope with high-altitude missions. Schematics illustrated the innovative bomb bay configuration that allowed for rapid release of ordnance with minimal aerodynamic disruption, a key factor in increasing bombing accuracy under hostile conditions.

Voices from the Cockpit

Yet no schematic could fully capture the visceral experience of flight. The true test of these revolutionary aircraft was written in the sky by the pilots who risked everything for a glimpse of freedom—and the promise of victory. Their accounts blend the cold precision of engineering with the raw emotion of aerial combat.

Captain Robert "Hawk" Henderson, a seasoned pilot who flew one of the experimental fighters, recalled his first encounter with a variable-geometry wing fighter:

> "The moment I took off in that new bird, it was as if the laws of physics had been rewritten. The wings swept back gracefully, cutting through the air like a knife. When I pushed the throttle, the engine roared, and I felt an exhilarating surge of power. It was both terrifying and liberating—like dancing on the edge of a razor."

For many pilots, the experimental bombers were equally awe-inspiring. Lieutenant Maria Delgado, who once piloted an advanced bomber prototype during a critical mission, described the experience in vivid detail:

> "Flying that bomber was unlike anything I had ever experienced. The cockpit was a marvel of design— controls that responded to the slightest touch and instruments that seemed almost alive. As we climbed to altitude, the roar of the engines melded with the rush of wind outside. But it wasn't just the speed that took my breath away—it was the sense of possibility. Up there, high above the chaos, I felt like I was part of something greater, a force that could change the course of the war."

Their narratives reveal not only the technical prowess of these machines but also the intimate connection between pilot and aircraft. In the cockpit, every adjustment to the throttle, every maneuver executed at breakneck speed, was both a technical act and a deeply personal moment of triumph or terror. The experimental designs transformed the experience of flight, imbuing it with an energy that defied description—a blend of raw power, precise control, and an almost spiritual communion with the elements.

The Duality of Innovation: Precision Meets Passion

The story of revolutionary aircraft design is, at its heart, a tale of duality. On one hand, there are the technical blueprints—cold, calculated, and painstakingly precise. On the other, there are the soaring, heart-pounding experiences of pilots who pushed these machines to their limits in real combat. The interplay between these two realms—engineering brilliance and human daring—created a dynamic that not only redefined aerial combat but also laid the groundwork for modern aviation.

Every technical breakthrough found its ultimate validation in the sky. The variable-geometry wings that reduced drag in theory had to prove their worth against enemy fire and turbulent weather. The enhanced powerplants and pressurized cockpits were subjected to the relentless forces of high-speed flight, where even a minor malfunction could spell disaster. And yet, with each mission flown, pilots and engineers refined these innovations, driven by a shared commitment to overcoming the impossible.

In these moments of airborne brilliance, the roar of the engine, the hum of advanced electronics, and the silent calculation of aerodynamic forces converged with the human senses—the tactile feel of the control stick, the adrenaline surge at each rapid maneuver, and the silent, determined focus in the face of danger. It was a synthesis of art and science, where every flight was both a technical demonstration and a profound, personal odyssey.

Beyond the Horizon

As experimental fighters and bombers began to make their mark on the skies, they not only changed the tactics of war but also the very essence of aerial combat. The innovations developed in those early days—steeped in both ingenuity and raw human courage—ushered in an era where speed, agility, and adaptability became the defining characteristics of air superiority.

The blueprints that once filled secret vaults now serve as a historical record of a time when the sky was transformed into a laboratory of possibility. And the voices of those who flew these experimental machines continue to echo, reminding us that the relentless pursuit of innovation is as much about human passion as it is about technical mastery.

In the dance of clouds and contrails, the revolutionary aircraft of World War II not only carved new paths through the air but also through the annals of history. Their legacy endures in every modern fighter and bomber—a tribute to a time when the sky became a canvas for both precision engineering and the indomitable spirit of flight.

Chapter 8: Rocket Pioneers – The Birth of Guided Missiles

Few innovations in military history have combined the raw force of technology with the heavy burden of human emotion as starkly as the early development of guided missiles. In World War II, the emergence of the V-1 and V-2 rockets not only changed the face of warfare but also forced engineers, scientists, and soldiers to confront the terrifying power of these new weapons. In this chapter, we take an in-depth look at the technical evolution and battlefield deployment of these early rockets, interlacing detailed schematics and engineering challenges with the raw emotional stakes felt by those who built—and faced—their unprecedented destructive potential.

The Dawn of Rocketry

The modern era of rocketry was born out of desperation and scientific ambition. As traditional artillery and bombers struggled to keep pace with evolving enemy defenses, visionaries on both sides of the conflict turned their gaze upward, seeking to harness the raw energy of rocket propulsion. The pioneering work that would eventually give rise to the V-1 and V-2 rockets began in secret laboratories and remote testing grounds, where every calculation, every prototype, was imbued with both hope and a palpable sense of dread.

Engineers were tasked with solving problems that had never before been tackled on such a massive scale. How could one reliably propel a projectile over long distances? How could guidance systems be integrated into a missile in an era when even the most advanced computing was in its infancy?

These were not merely technical questions—they were existential challenges that carried the weight of a nation's survival.

The V-1: The Buzz Bomb

The V-1 rocket, often dubbed the "buzz bomb" due to the distinctive droning sound of its pulsejet engine, was one of the first guided missiles to see combat. Its design was deceptively simple: a fixed-wing aircraft powered by a pulsejet engine, capable of delivering a small, but devastating, payload. Detailed technical blueprints reveal a compact, aerodynamic structure designed for rapid mass production. Its guidance system, rudimentary by today's standards, relied on preset flight paths and simple control surfaces—a far cry from the precision of modern missiles, yet revolutionary in its time.

For the soldiers and civilians who first heard the ominous hum of a V-1, the experience was terrifying. The buzz of the engine heralded not only the impending impact of a physical explosion but also the realization that warfare was evolving into a domain where machines could be unleashed with little warning, guided by the unseen hand of technology. An engineer from the development team recalled,

> "We knew our creation was imperfect—a crude harbinger of what

could be. Yet every test run brought with it a mix of pride and horror. We had set in motion a new era of mechanized terror, one that would forever blur the lines between scientific progress and moral consequence."

The V-2: The Wunderwaffe

While the V-1 represented the first step, the V-2 rocket would become a true game-changer. As the world's first long-range guided ballistic missile, the V-2 was a masterpiece of engineering that pushed the boundaries of what was technically possible. Powered by a liquid-fueled engine and featuring advanced guidance systems, the V-2 could travel at supersonic speeds, reaching altitudes and ranges that left traditional defenses helpless. Schematics from its development reveal intricate details: a combustion chamber designed to withstand extreme temperatures, precision-machined components to ensure aerodynamic stability, and gyroscopic systems that attempted to steer the missile on a predetermined course.

The emotional toll on those who engineered the V-2 was immense. Working in isolated, secretive facilities, many scientists wrestled with the duality of their work: the pursuit of scientific advancement on one hand, and the devastating potential of their creations on the other. A lead engineer, haunted by the implications of his work, later confessed,

> "Every calculation, every test, felt like walking a razor's edge between genius and destruction. We were building a weapon that could erase cities in minutes—a machine that carried the cold logic of mathematics and the weight of human lives in its wake."

The V-2's deployment on the battlefields of Europe marked a turning point. Its ability to deliver a sudden, unpredictable strike transformed the strategic landscape, instilling terror in civilian populations and forcing military planners to reconsider the very nature of defense. The rocket's impact was felt not only in its physical devastation but in the psychological shock it sent rippling across nations.

Engineering and Emotional Struggles

Behind every blueprint and test flight was a team of individuals grappling with extraordinary pressure. In the sterile confines of research bunkers and bombed-out hangars, engineers worked around the clock to refine their designs. Their laboratories were filled with the whir of machinery, the scratch of pen on paper, and the constant hum of anxious debate.

In these environments, technical challenges were interwoven with ethical quandaries.

For many, the realization that their innovations could cause widespread devastation was a source of deep personal conflict. The relentless drive to perfect a missile system was matched only by the heavy burden of knowing that, in the wrong hands, their work could lead to catastrophic loss of life. The engineers' emotions were as volatile as the fuels they worked with—ranging from fervent nationalistic pride to profound moral ambivalence. One scientist, whose later reflections became emblematic of the era, noted,

> "We were caught between the promise of a technological leap forward and the nightmare of its consequences. Every successful test was bittersweet—a triumph of human ingenuity shadowed by the knowledge of the lives it might one day end."

Deployment and Battlefield Impact

The deployment of the V-1 and V-2 rockets marked a seismic shift in the conduct of war. When these guided missiles were unleashed, the battlefield extended beyond the terrestrial realm into the vast, unpredictable expanse of the sky. Their sudden arrival disrupted established military strategies and forced commanders to adopt new defensive measures. No longer confined to the predictable arcs of artillery, the rockets introduced an element of randomness and fear that reshaped strategic planning.

Frontline accounts vividly capture the impact of these weapons. Civilians in bombed-out cities described the unsettling silence that would descend moments before a rocket's arrival, followed by an ear-splitting roar and a burst of light that obliterated everything in its path. Soldiers, trained to recognize the telltale signs of an incoming missile, spoke of the adrenaline surge that accompanied each alert—a mix of terror, determination, and the grim acceptance of war's new realities.

For those on the receiving end, the rockets were more than just instruments of destruction—they were harbingers of a future where technology could both save and end lives in an instant. The psychological impact was profound; every whir of an engine or flash of light in the distance carried with it the potential to alter the course of an entire community.

The Dual Legacy of Rocket Pioneers

The birth of guided missiles during World War II stands as a testament to both human ingenuity and its capacity for destruction. The technical breakthroughs that led to the V-1 and V-2 rockets opened new frontiers in aerospace engineering, laying the groundwork for modern missile technology and space exploration. Yet, they also served as stark reminders of the heavy moral cost of innovation—a cost measured in both human lives and the enduring scars of warfare.

The legacy of these rocket pioneers is a complex tapestry woven from threads of brilliant engineering, relentless ambition, and profound ethical introspection. The detailed schematics and rigorous tests that once filled confidential reports now serve as historical documents, illuminating the rapid pace of technological advancement and the enduring impact of these weapons on military strategy.

In the hearts and minds of those who engineered and faced these early guided missiles, there remains a bittersweet understanding: the same ingenuity that propelled humanity toward the stars could also unleash untold devastation. This duality—of promise and peril, of progress shadowed by its consequences—continues to shape our collective understanding of technology and war.

• • •

Chapter 9: Naval Novelties – Reinventing Underwater Warfare

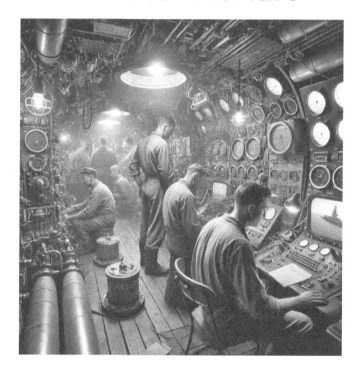

In the shadowed depths of World War II, a hidden battle unfolded beneath the waves. As surface fleets clashed and aerial assaults rained down from above, the underwater realm became a theater of innovation and adaptation. Naval engineers and daring submariners alike were compelled to reinvent the tools of maritime warfare. In this chapter, we explore the creative adaptations in submarine design and the transformation of warships, all while painting a vivid, sensory portrait of life beneath the waves and aboard cramped, reimagined decks.

The Evolution of Underwater Craft

Traditional naval design, rooted in decades of surface combat, could no longer address the stealth and resilience required in modern warfare. In response, engineers began to craft submarines and modified warships that were as much marvels of engineering as they were symbols of defiance against overwhelming odds.

- **Streamlined Hulls and Pressure-Resistant Materials:**
  The submarines of this era were refashioned with sleek, hydrodynamic hulls designed to slice silently through the water. Reinforced with new, pressure-resistant alloys, these vessels could dive deeper and remain undetected for longer periods. Blueprints from secret naval projects reveal intricate calculations: curvature lines optimized to reduce drag, bulkheads reinforced with innovative composite

materials, and specially designed propeller systems engineered for near-silent operation.

- **Enhanced Sonar and Stealth Technologies:**
  Beyond structural improvements, advancements in sonar technology enabled these underwater warriors to detect enemy ships without revealing their own presence. Experimental sound-dampening materials and vibration-reducing engines were integrated into submarine designs, turning each vessel into a ghostly predator of the deep. These adaptations allowed for more precise navigation in treacherous waters, where every decibel could be the difference between survival and detection.

- **Reimagined Warship Modifications:**
  On the surface, warships were not left untouched by innovation. Frantic modifications saw battleships and cruisers outfitted with additional anti-aircraft guns, reinforced decks, and even hastily converted radar systems. These changes, though often improvised under the pressure of imminent attack, served to prolong the operational life of vessels that might otherwise have succumbed to the evolving threats of modern combat.

Life Below the Surface: A Sensory Journey

To truly understand the transformative nature of these naval novelties, one must venture beneath the surface and into the confined, often claustrophobic world of a submarine. Life underwater was a study in contrasts—a blend of silent, eerie calm punctuated by sudden, heart-stopping moments of intense action.

- **A World of Muted Hues and Enclosed Spaces:**
  Inside a submarine, space was at a premium. The decks were narrow and the corridors dimly lit by the glow of instrument panels and emergency lamps. Every surface, from the cold metal walls to the scuffed linoleum floors, bore the marks of constant use and desperate adaptation. The air was heavy with the scent of engine oil and the faint, ever-present tang of seawater—a constant reminder of the vessel's immersion in an unforgiving environment.

- **The Soundscape of the Deep:**
  Underwater, the usual clamor of battle was replaced by a profound silence—a silence occasionally broken by the low, rhythmic hum of the engines and the distant, almost imperceptible creaks of the pressure hull.

For the crew, this quiet was both a blessing and a curse. It provided a temporary respite from the chaos of surface warfare, yet it also amplified every minor noise—a whisper of movement, the soft tap of a tool against metal—each sound a potential harbinger of enemy detection.

- **Tactile and Emotional Realities:** The physicality of life at sea was defined by its limitations. In cramped quarters, every inch of space was precious. Crew members learned to adapt, sharing sleeping bunks and personal mementos in tight quarters. The tactile sensations were acute: the cold, smooth feel of a metal railing, the rough texture of a patched-up deck, and the relentless pressure of the deep pressing in from all sides. Each dive was a visceral reminder of both the power of nature and the ingenuity of those who dared to conquer it.

Voices from the Depths

The true measure of these innovations lies in the experiences of the men who lived and fought beneath the waves. Their accounts weave together technical achievements with raw, personal emotion:

"The first time our new submarine dove below the surface, it felt like entering another world entirely," recalled Lieutenant Markus, a veteran of numerous covert missions. "Down there, the silence is overwhelming—a profound quiet that makes you hyper-aware of every creak and groan of the vessel. But it's also a sanctuary, a place where we could outmaneuver our enemies. Every adjustment to the controls, every whispered order, was a reminder of the delicate balance between innovation and survival."

In another intimate recollection, Ensign Lydia described the sensory impact of a prolonged underwater patrol:

"Spending days in a submarine is like living inside a heartbeat. The constant hum of the engines, the subtle vibrations through the deck—it becomes a rhythm you can almost feel in your bones. The air, recycled and tinged with the ocean's salt, is a constant companion. You learn to cherish even the smallest comforts—a hot cup of tea, a shared laugh over a makeshift meal. It's a life of extremes, but also of profound camaraderie and resilience."

The Legacy of Naval Innovation

The creative adaptations in submarine design and the modifications of warships during World War II were more than just tactical necessities; they were transformative innovations that reshaped naval warfare. These vessels, born from the crucible of desperate need and brilliant ingenuity, extended the reach of military strategy far beyond the surface. Their design principles not only allowed for new methods of engagement but also set the stage for modern underwater technology and stealth operations.

The legacy of these innovations endures in every modern submarine and stealth warship—a tribute to the courage and resourcefulness of those who, in the depths of uncertainty, found a way to redefine the rules of engagement. Their story is a testament to the enduring spirit of innovation, a reminder that even in the most confined and challenging environments, human ingenuity can chart a course toward a new horizon.

Chapter 10: Deception by Design – The Art of the Dummy

In a war where every advantage was fiercely contested, deception emerged as a weapon as potent as any blade or bullet. The creation and strategic deployment of decoy tanks, aircraft, and installations became a critical facet of wartime ingenuity—designed not to confront the enemy head-on but to mislead, confuse, and ultimately neutralize their efforts. In this chapter, we analyze how these "dummy" assets were conceived, engineered, and deployed, and we interlace technical details with firsthand operative reports that reveal the deep psychological impact these deceptions had on enemy forces.

Crafting the Illusion

Traditional military hardware had long been the backbone of combat, but as reconnaissance technology improved, so too did the need to outwit the enemy by creating convincing forgeries of war machines. Engineers and designers began to repurpose everyday materials and obsolete equipment into decoys that mimicked the appearance and even some of the operational characteristics of real tanks, aircraft, and fortifications.

- **Decoy Tanks:**
  Hollow replicas constructed from wood, canvas, and metal scraps were painted and assembled to simulate the imposing profile of armored vehicles. Detailed blueprints show that designers paid meticulous attention to proportions, shadow effects, and even the slight wear typical of battle-hardened tanks. These dummy tanks were often positioned in formations that mirrored active units, creating the illusion of

reinforced lines where none actually
existed.

- **Fake Aircraft:**
  To mislead enemy aerial reconnaissance,
  large-scale models of fighter planes and
  bombers were erected in fields or along
  runways. Some of these decoys even
  incorporated rudimentary moving parts—
  such as rotating propellers powered by wind
  or simple motorized systems—to enhance
  their realism. The visual fidelity was critical;
  aerial photographs needed to be
  indistinguishable from genuine combat
  aircraft to effectively deter enemy targeting.

- **Decoy Installations:**
  Beyond vehicles, entire installations—
  including anti-aircraft batteries, command
  posts, and radar stations—were simulated
  using inflatable structures, plywood facades,
  and cleverly arranged camouflage nets. The
  goal was to create a comprehensive picture
  of military strength that forced adversaries
  to divert resources to reconnaissance and
  potential strikes against phantom targets.

Strategic Deployment and Tactical Impact

The deployment of these dummy assets was a
deliberate and meticulously planned operation.
Commanders recognized that in modern warfare,

information was as valuable as firepower, and every false lead could divert enemy resources and attention.

Field commanders orchestrated entire "phantom" divisions, using decoys to create the impression of an armored concentration or a fortified airbase. These deceptions were often coordinated with electronic countermeasures and radio traffic designed to mimic normal operations. In one notable operation, a series of decoy tanks was positioned near a river crossing, leading the enemy to believe that a major armored assault was imminent. The result was a costly diversion of enemy troops and armored units, which were left vulnerable in other sectors.

Operative Reports: The Psychological Warfare of Deception

The true power of these deceptions was not measured solely by their technical sophistication, but by the profound psychological impact they exerted on enemy forces. Operative reports and firsthand accounts paint a vivid picture of confusion and disarray among adversaries confronted with the artifice of war:

"Our intelligence operators reported multiple instances where enemy reconnaissance was thrown off course by what appeared to be entire battalions of tanks—only to discover later that these were nothing more than dummies, standing silently in the mist," reported Captain Armand, a liaison officer in a strategic deception unit.

Another report from a frontline observer detailed the impact on enemy morale:

"I could see the hesitation in their ranks, the uncertainty in their movements. They were second-guessing every photograph and every radar blip. It was as if the very presence of these decoys sapped their confidence. Each false lead was a blow to their planning and a testament to our ability to control the narrative of battle."

Such reports underscore that the decoys did more than merely misdirect—they instilled doubt, disrupted enemy decision-making, and often forced a defensive posture where aggressive action might have been expected.

The Art and Science of Deception

Blending art with military science, the creation of dummy assets required a deep understanding of both visual perception and enemy psychology. Designers collaborated closely with field commanders, ensuring that every decoy was positioned to maximize its impact. The interplay of natural light, shadow, and camouflage was studied as rigorously as ballistics and engine performance. Technical schematics were annotated not only with material specifications but also with guidelines for optimal placement—suggesting, for example, the best angles from which a decoy tank would appear most convincing to an enemy observer.

In the world of deception, every detail mattered. The sound of distant, non-existent engines was mimicked by low-frequency speakers hidden nearby, and occasional bursts of fake radio chatter were transmitted to add an extra layer of realism. The goal was to craft a holistic illusion, one that could stand up to both technological scrutiny and the gut instincts of experienced enemy scouts.

A Legacy of Illusion

The strategic use of decoys during World War II represented a turning point in the art of deception.

These dummy assets not only saved countless lives by diverting enemy fire and resources but also reshaped military doctrine regarding the value of misdirection. The success of these operations has since influenced modern tactics in electronic warfare, cyber deception, and psychological operations. Today, the legacy of these early decoys endures as a powerful reminder that in warfare, as in life, sometimes the greatest strength lies in the ability to make others believe what isn't real.

In the interplay of light and shadow on a battle-scarred landscape, the art of the dummy stands as a testament to the creativity and audacity of those who dared to deceive an enemy through the power of illusion. Every decoy tank, every fake aircraft, every simulated installation was more than a clever ruse—it was a statement that, in war, the mind can be as formidable a weapon as any steel or fire.

Chapter 11: Guerrilla Ingenuity – Improvised Weapons of Resistance

In the shadow of occupying forces and the relentless drumbeat of war, the resourcefulness of local militias and insurgent groups shone as a beacon of defiance. With conventional arsenals out of reach and supply lines severed by enemy might, these fighters turned the very remnants of a shattered society into weapons of resistance. In this chapter, we explore how necessity bred ingenious, improvised weapons and tactics, blending rigorous technical adaptations with deeply personal stories of courage and resourcefulness in the face of overwhelming odds.

From Scrap to Strike: The Technical Alchemy of Improvisation

In environments where access to manufactured weaponry was limited, ingenuity became the lifeblood of resistance. In hidden workshops, basements, and even repurposed ruins, local fighters set about transforming everyday materials into deadly instruments of war.

- **Homemade Mortars and Artillery:**
  With little more than scrap metal, discarded pipes, and remnants of industrial equipment, insurgents engineered rudimentary mortars. Field schematics—detailed on crumpled notepads and scrawled on smudged maps—reveal the careful calculations that went into harnessing chemical reactions to propel improvised shells. These makeshift devices, while lacking the refinement of factory-

produced ordnance, provided a critical edge in ambushes and defensive actions, often catching enemy units off guard.

- **Explosive Devices and Booby Traps:** Using readily available chemicals and components salvaged from bombed-out factories or abandoned vehicles, guerrilla fighters assembled improvised explosive devices (IEDs) with startling effectiveness. Diagrams captured on hastily drafted blueprints showed layered fusing systems—tripwires interlaced with pressure plates and simple timer circuits—that turned everyday locations into lethal minefields. In the hands of insurgents, even a common door or a seemingly innocuous rock could become a trigger for chaos.

- **Adapted Firearms and Hybrid Weapons:** The creative spirit extended to small arms as well. Outdated or captured rifles were often modified with custom attachments: makeshift scopes crafted from repurposed glass, reconfigured triggers for faster response, and even hybrid weapons combining parts of different firearms to create a new, more effective tool. Field manuals, passed hand-to-hand among resistance groups, documented these modifications in a language that was as technical as it was pragmatic, emphasizing ease of repair and adaptability under fire.

- **Improvised Defensive Mechanisms:**
  Beyond offensive weapons, insurgents also developed ingenious defensive measures. Camouflaged barriers constructed from sandbags, debris, and even locally sourced vegetation were arranged to funnel enemy movements into kill zones. Sound traps—simple devices that mimicked the noise of approaching forces—were deployed to misdirect enemy patrols or alert fighters to impending danger.

The Tactical Art of Improvised Warfare

The creativity of guerrilla warfare was not limited to the construction of weapons; it was embedded in every tactical decision. Lacking the mass and firepower of conventional armies, insurgents relied on speed, stealth, and surprise to turn the tide in their favor.

- **Hit-and-Run Ambushes:**
  By leveraging the element of surprise, small bands of fighters executed lightning-quick ambushes. Utilizing terrain to their advantage, they would deploy improvised mortars or IEDs along known enemy routes. The resulting explosions—often timed to coincide with the enemy's moment of greatest vulnerability—brought both

physical damage and a crippling
psychological blow.

- **Decentralized and Adaptive Operations:**
  Without a centralized command structure,
  each guerrilla unit operated with remarkable
  autonomy. Adaptability was key; units
  tailored their weapons and tactics to the
  specific challenges of their environment,
  whether in dense urban ruins or sprawling,
  rugged countryside. This flexibility allowed
  them to quickly modify plans in response to
  enemy movements and shifting battlefield
  conditions.
- **Psychological Warfare Through
  Deception:**
  Every improvised weapon and ambush was
  as much a psychological tactic as a physical
  one. The constant threat of unseen
  dangers—hidden traps, unexpected mortar
  fire, or reconfigured firearms—instilled a
  pervasive sense of uncertainty in enemy
  ranks. The fear of the unknown often forced
  conventional forces into a defensive
  posture, sapping their morale and disrupting
  their strategies.

Voices from the Resistance: Personal Stories of Bravery

The human element in guerrilla warfare is best
understood through the first-hand accounts of those

who risked everything in defiance of oppression. Their voices echo across time, revealing the profound blend of technical ingenuity and raw courage that defined their struggle.

"In the dead of night, we huddled in a cellar with nothing but the scraps of metal from a collapsed warehouse. With trembling hands and a determination born of desperation, we rigged together a mortar from pipes and old car parts. Every explosion we heard was a reminder that our survival depended on turning the enemy's own might against them. It was crude, but it was our lifeline."
— Pierre, a French partisan

In the rugged, mist-shrouded forests of Eastern Europe, insurgent groups honed their craft on rugged terrain:

"We didn't have the luxury of fancy equipment. Every tripwire, every booby trap, had to be improvised with what we had—sometimes a simple nail, sometimes an old battery. The fear was constant, but with every successful ambush, our resolve grew. It wasn't just about the weapons; it was about the message: we would not be

defeated by our circumstances."
— Milica, Yugoslav partisan

Another stirring account from a makeshift armorer in a besieged village underscores the intimate link between innovation and survival:

> "I spent nights under the faint glow of a kerosene lamp, reworking old rifles and combining parts that were never meant to fit together. Each modification, however small, was a triumph over the oppression that sought to strip us of our dignity. Every adjusted trigger and reconfigured barrel was a silent defiance—a testament to our refusal to surrender."
> — An anonymous insurgent armorer

The Legacy of Guerrilla Ingenuity

The improvised weapons and unconventional tactics of guerrilla fighters during World War II were born out of necessity but left an indelible mark on military strategy. Their ability to transform everyday materials into instruments of resistance has inspired countless subsequent movements and remains a potent reminder of the power of human creativity in the face of overwhelming odds.

Every homemade mortar, every cleverly rigged IED, and every adapted firearm represented more than a tactical innovation—they embodied the spirit of resistance, the belief that even the smallest act of defiance could alter the course of history. In the harshest conditions, where formal supply lines were a luxury and every moment was a fight for survival, these fighters forged a legacy of resourcefulness that continues to resonate in the annals of unconventional warfare.

Their technical innovations, detailed in tattered manuals and passed down through whispered instructions in hidden camps, illustrate a fundamental truth: when pushed to the brink, the human spirit can convert the debris of destruction into a tool for liberation. The legacy of guerrilla ingenuity is not merely one of improvised weaponry, but of a resilient defiance that transformed despair into hope and desperation into triumph.

As the echoes of their struggles persist, the stories of Pierre, Milica, and countless unnamed heroes remind us that in the darkest of times, the ingenuity of the human spirit can ignite a flame of resistance that burns brighter than any manufactured weapon.

Chapter 12: Crafting Perception – The Tactics of Psychological Warfare

In the theater of war, where brute force often meets its match in ingenuity, perception itself became a battlefield. Beyond the clash of arms and the roar of engines, a quieter yet no less potent struggle unfolded—the war of ideas, emotions, and deception. In this chapter, we explore how propaganda, staged spectacles, and deliberate misinformation were marshaled to alter the enemy's sense of reality, turning uncertainty into a weapon. Through carefully orchestrated displays and subtle manipulations, commanders sought to sow discord, induce hesitation, and shatter the enemy's resolve long before the first shot was fired.

The Power of Propaganda

At the heart of psychological warfare lay the art of propaganda. Governments and military leaders recognized early on that controlling the narrative could shape the outcome of conflicts. Posters, radio broadcasts, and clandestine leaflets painted a picture of invincibility and righteousness. These messages were crafted not only to bolster the morale of one's own troops but also to undermine the confidence of the adversary.

- **Emotive Imagery and Rousing Slogans:** Propaganda campaigns employed vivid images of heroism, sacrifice, and triumph, interwoven with slogans designed to inspire and intimidate. Photographs of determined soldiers, iconic landmarks shrouded in patriotic fervor, and dramatic renderings of the enemy depicted as monstrous and weak were disseminated widely. Every poster, every broadcast, was an invitation to believe in a narrative where victory was not only possible but inevitable.

- **The Internet Before the Internet:** Long before digital media, the power of word-of-mouth and printed materials was harnessed to create an undercurrent of doubt in enemy ranks. Secret pamphlets and underground newspapers offered alternative realities—stories of impossible victories, exaggerated losses, and heroic last stands—that blurred the line between fact and fiction. In the fog of war, where communication was as much about emotion as it was about information, these messages could turn hope into despair, and vice versa.

Staged Spectacles and Deceptive Displays

The battlefield was not solely a realm of physical combat—it was also a stage on which grand illusions were performed. Military strategists understood that a well-timed spectacle could divert enemy attention, deplete their resources, and disrupt their plans.

- **Phantom Armies and Illusory Fortresses:** In one remarkable campaign, decoy units were deployed to simulate the presence of massive forces in strategic locations.

Dummy tanks and fake artillery batteries, meticulously constructed and positioned, created the illusion of overwhelming strength. Enemy reconnaissance images captured these phantasmal formations, leading to costly misallocations of resources as they prepared for battles that were never to be fought.

- **The Deceptive Calm Before the Storm:** Perhaps the most chilling aspect of these staged displays was the eerie, calculated calm that preceded an assault. Commanders would engineer prolonged periods of quiet—an almost supernatural silence—before unleashing a barrage of coordinated strikes. In those moments of stillness, the enemy's nerves frayed. They stood waiting, uncertain whether the quiet was a sign of impending doom or a trap designed to lull them into complacency. The silence itself became a weapon—a deceptive calm that magnified the shock when the storm finally broke.

Misinformation: Shaping Reality with Lies

Deliberate misinformation was another key tool in the psychological arsenal. By seeding false intelligence and creating conflicting narratives, military leaders could confuse and paralyze enemy decision-making.

- **Counterintelligence and Double Agents:** Through a network of spies and double agents, falsified reports and counterfeit orders were disseminated within enemy ranks. These carefully crafted messages led opposing commanders to question the reliability of their own intelligence, sowing seeds of paranoia and distrust. When uncertainty reigned supreme, even the best-laid plans could unravel.
- **Echoes of False Hope and Dire Warning:** In some instances, misinformation painted an overly optimistic picture of an impending offensive, causing enemy forces to lower their guard. In others, it delivered grim warnings of overwhelming force that never materialized, triggering premature withdrawals and tactical disarray. The psychological impact was profound— soldiers, isolated in the fog of uncertainty, began to doubt not only their strategies but also their own senses.

Voices from the Front: Operative Insights

The true measure of psychological warfare is best understood through the voices of those who experienced its effects firsthand. Operative reports and personal recollections capture the essence of deception at its most raw and transformative:

> "In the silence before an attack, it felt as if time itself had stopped—a stillness so profound that every heartbeat echoed like a drum. We knew something was coming, but we never could be sure what. That eerie calm, that suspenseful quiet, was the enemy's greatest weapon. It turned our own thoughts against us, making us doubt even our strongest convictions."
> — Major Alain Dubois, a veteran of deceptive operations

Another operative recalled the bitter irony of misinformation:

> "There were days when our own intelligence was a jumbled mess of truth and lies. We received orders based on information that we later learned was fabricated. It was like trying to navigate through a mirror maze—each reflection distorted, each step laden with uncertainty. The psychological toll was immense; the line between friend and foe blurred in our minds, leaving us in a perpetual state of vigilance and doubt."

— Lieutenant Sara Varga, intelligence officer

These firsthand accounts illustrate that the tactics of psychological warfare were not merely abstract strategies—they were lived experiences that reshaped the very fabric of combat, leaving lasting impressions on all who encountered them.

The Enduring Impact of Shaping Perception

The legacy of psychological warfare endures long after the last battle has been fought. The techniques developed during World War II laid the groundwork for modern strategies in information warfare and strategic deception. Propaganda, staged spectacles, and misinformation have since evolved with technology, but the fundamental principles remain the same: control the narrative, disrupt the enemy's perception, and strike at the heart of their confidence.

In the interplay of light and shadow on the battlefield, the art of crafting perception remains a powerful reminder that in war, the mind is as important a battleground as any physical terrain. The eerie calm before a deceptive storm, the carefully orchestrated dance of truth and lie—these are the instruments that, when wielded with precision, can turn the tide of conflict without a single bullet being fired.

Chapter 13: The Science of Sabotage – Hidden Engineering Feats

In the covert corridors of war, far from the glare of front-line battles, a silent revolution was underway. Beneath the enemy's nose and hidden within the rubble of occupied cities, engineers and technicians labored in secret workshops, forging unconventional combat tools designed to undermine the war machine from within. In this chapter, we delve into the clandestine world of sabotage—a realm where the precision of technical schematics met the raw urgency of survival, and where every bolt tightened and circuit soldered carried the weight of hope and defiance.

The Covert Laboratories of Innovation

Behind shuttered doors and in repurposed basements, these hidden workshops became sanctuaries of subversion. Here, the engineers worked under constant threat of discovery, their activities shrouded in secrecy. Maps marked with coded locations and faded blueprints passed discreetly between trusted hands, each document a testament to the ingenuity and courage required to strike at the enemy from the shadows.

- **Secret Schematics and Makeshift Designs:**
  Detailed sketches, often drawn by hand on scrap paper, outlined the design of devices that could disable enemy communications, disrupt supply lines, or even disable armored vehicles from within. One set of schematics, for instance, described a compact yet potent electromagnetic pulse (EMP) generator. Its design incorporated

salvaged radio components, repurposed capacitors, and a finely tuned oscillator—a delicate balance of physics and engineering intended to neutralize enemy electronics without causing indiscriminate collateral damage. Annotations in the margins read, "Test under minimal load to avoid detection," highlighting both the technical precision and the high stakes involved.

- **Innovative Sabotage Devices:** Other projects included remotely detonated time bombs, ingeniously concealed within everyday objects, and cutting tools designed to weaken critical infrastructure components such as fuel pipelines and armored vehicle treads. These devices were built with an emphasis on simplicity and reliability—often using easily available materials to ensure that, even in the event of supply shortages, the sabotage effort could continue unabated.

Engineering Feats Under Fire

The science of sabotage was not merely a technical challenge; it was an act of defiance. Every engineered device represented a quiet rebellion against oppression, a strategic disruption meticulously planned and executed under the constant threat of enemy reprisals.

- **Precision Under Pressure:**
  In one clandestine operation, a team of technicians developed a miniature drilling device capable of compromising the structural integrity of enemy bunkers. The device's blueprint, etched in fine lines on a single sheet of paper, detailed a compact motor assembly, a series of rotating carbide bits, and a battery pack ingeniously derived from repurposed automotive components. Every measurement was critical, and every component had to function flawlessly under pressure—a true engineering marvel born in the crucible of necessity.

- **Adaptive Innovations:**
  Sabotage often required adapting to ever-changing enemy technologies. As enemy vehicles became more fortified, engineers responded with modified explosive charges and cutting torches that could slice through reinforced armor. Field notes chronicled adjustments made on the fly: "Increase fuse length by 0.5 seconds to synchronize with engine cycle," or "Use alternative alloy for heat shielding when standard materials run low." These records, though informal, served as vital guides for subsequent missions, ensuring that the cycle of innovation continued unabated despite harsh conditions.

Voices from the Hidden Workshops

The engineers who risked everything in these secret workshops carried the burden of both technical challenges and moral dilemmas. Their personal reflections provide a window into the soul of sabotage—a blend of scientific rigor and heartfelt defiance.

> "Every time I picked up my soldering iron, I knew I was not just building a device—I was building a chance for freedom. In our dimly lit room, with only the hum of old generators to keep us company, every circuit we completed was a silent strike against tyranny."
> — Anatoly, a covert technician working in an underground workshop beneath a bombed-out factory

Another stirring account comes from Maria, an engineer whose work on disabling enemy communication lines saved countless lives:

> "The pressure was relentless. We had to design something that was both simple and deadly effective— something that wouldn't draw attention until it was too late. I remember the long nights, the weight of knowing that

our success could mean the difference between life and death. Every miscalculation was a risk, but every breakthrough was a spark of hope in the darkness."
— Maria, clandestine communications specialist

These voices remind us that the science of sabotage was as much about human resilience and moral conviction as it was about technical prowess. In the hidden world of secret workshops, every prototype was a beacon of resistance—a reminder that even in the most oppressive circumstances, ingenuity could flourish.

The Ripple Effect of Hidden Feats

The impact of these clandestine engineering feats extended far beyond the immediate tactical advantages. By undermining enemy operations from within, the sabotage efforts forced the adversary into a state of perpetual uncertainty. Every malfunctioning communication system, every disabled piece of equipment, and every unexpected explosion contributed to a broader strategy of eroding the enemy's confidence and operational capacity.

The legacy of these hidden engineering feats lives on in modern approaches to asymmetric warfare. The techniques honed in those secret workshops— rapid prototyping, adaptive problem-solving, and the relentless pursuit of innovation under duress— continue to influence military strategy and inspire new generations of engineers dedicated to the art of subversion.

In the dim corridors of secret workshops and behind layers of coded secrecy, the science of sabotage emerged as a silent, powerful force. It was here, in the interplay of technical precision and raw human emotion, that the seeds of modern covert operations were sown. The devices engineered in those hidden sanctuaries not only disrupted enemy plans but also illuminated a path of resistance, proving that even under the most oppressive circumstances, the spirit of innovation could blaze a trail toward liberation.

Chapter 14: Ambush and Surprise – Unorthodox Battlefield Tactics

In the theater of war, not every victory was won by overwhelming force. Often, the most decisive moments arose from split-second decisions—a well-timed ambush, an unexpected maneuver—that rippled through the larger strategy of a campaign.

This chapter chronicles the creative ambush strategies and unorthodox battlefield tactics that shifted battle outcomes. It juxtaposes the adrenaline-fueled immediacy of in-the-moment decisions with their far-reaching, long-term strategic impact.

The Anatomy of an Ambush

Ambushes are the art of turning the enemy's momentum against them. In many instances, commanders and small units meticulously planned ambushes that relied on stealth, surprise, and the effective use of terrain. Rather than confronting a well-prepared enemy head-on, these forces chose to strike from hidden positions—often in dense forests, along narrow mountain passes, or in the urban labyrinth of ruined cities.

- **Terrain as an Ally:**
  Commanders scouted for natural chokepoints where enemy vehicles and infantry would be forced to slow down. Hidden by the landscape—be it thick foliage or the crumbling remains of a city block— ambushers waited patiently. Every rustle in the underbrush and every echo of distant artillery fire heightened the tension, transforming these quiet moments into the calm before a sudden, violent storm.

- **Deceptive Positions and Camouflage:**
  Utilizing camouflage nets, locally sourced
  materials, and even captured enemy
  uniforms, guerrilla forces and specialized
  units would blend into their surroundings.
  Their positions were often so well concealed
  that even seasoned enemy scouts could
  mistake them for natural features of the
  landscape. Detailed reconnaissance maps
  and firsthand accounts reveal how these
  forces prepared trap-like setups: hidden
  machine gun nests, concealed sniper
  positions, and improvised explosive traps
  meticulously coordinated to trigger in
  unison.

Split-Second Decisions Under Fire

The success of an ambush frequently hinged on
the ability of soldiers to react instantly. In the chaos
of battle, every heartbeat counted, and decisions
had to be made in the blink of an eye.
Commanders often spoke of the "magic moment"—
that singular instant when the enemy, caught
completely off guard, was forced into a
disorganized retreat or, worse, a rout.

> "I remember the moment our unit
> sprang the ambush," recalled
> Lieutenant Marco, a veteran of several

covert operations. "One second, we were hidden, barely breathing, and the next, the silence shattered as we opened fire. It was a chaos of gunfire, shouts, and the screech of tires as enemy vehicles careened into obstacles. In that split second, our training took over, and every decision was a blend of instinct and precise timing. It was a microcosm of war itself."

— Lieutenant Marco, frontline commander

These rapid decisions not only dictated the immediate outcome of the engagement but also set the stage for the longer-term strategic impact. An ambush that effectively crippled a key enemy unit could delay reinforcements, disrupt supply lines, and sow doubt among higher command ranks.

Unexpected Maneuvers That Changed the Game

Beyond traditional ambushes, unorthodox maneuvers became critical to adapting to evolving battlefield dynamics. These tactics were as diverse as the environments in which they were deployed:

- **Nighttime Raids and Sudden Withdrawals:**

Under the cover of darkness, some units would launch sudden raids on enemy outposts or supply depots. Using the chaos of low visibility to their advantage, they struck swiftly and then melted away into the shadows. The sudden nature of these attacks often left enemy forces scrambling to recover from disorientation, giving the attackers time to regroup and plan their next move.

- **Decoy Maneuvers and Feints:**
  In some cases, entire units were employed as decoys to divert enemy attention from the real point of attack. By staging a feint—a simulated assault at one location—commanders could force the enemy to redistribute their forces. Meanwhile, the main attack would be launched from an unexpected quarter. Such maneuvers required meticulous planning, with every element of timing and positioning orchestrated down to the last detail.

- **Rapid Flanking and Encirclement:**
  In fluid battle scenarios, small teams adept in mobile warfare would execute rapid flanking maneuvers, bypassing enemy strongholds to strike at vulnerable rear areas. These swift movements, often executed on foot or in lightly armored vehicles, demonstrated a level of flexibility that conventional forces struggled to match. When a flank attack succeeded, it could

lead to a rapid encirclement of enemy units, effectively turning their own formation against them.

The Long-Term Impact of Tactical Surprise

The immediate effects of an ambush or unexpected maneuver were evident in the chaos and confusion they induced. However, the strategic implications often unfolded over weeks or even months:

- **Disruption of Enemy Morale:**
  Repeated ambushes and unpredictable maneuvers forced enemy commanders to adopt a defensive mindset. The constant threat of sudden attacks eroded morale and instilled a sense of vulnerability, even among the most battle-hardened troops. Psychological reports from captured enemy officers reveal a pervasive sense of distrust and uncertainty about enemy movements.
- **Forcing Strategic Revisions:**
  Successful ambushes disrupted enemy logistics and forced them to reallocate resources to defensive positions. High command was compelled to revise their strategies, often diverting significant reserves to guard against further unexpected attacks. In one notable campaign, a series of well-coordinated

ambushes along a critical supply route forced an enemy division to delay a major offensive—a delay that proved pivotal in the overall war effort.

- **A Ripple Effect on Allied Tactics:** The effectiveness of unorthodox tactics inspired similar approaches among allied forces. As the success stories of ambushes and rapid maneuvers became widely known, they were studied and replicated in training exercises. The innovative spirit of these tactics helped to shape modern doctrines of asymmetrical warfare, where flexibility and surprise remain as crucial as raw firepower.

The Human Element: Courage and Calculated Risk

At the heart of these tactical innovations were the individuals who executed them. The courage required to step into the unknown, to trust in a plan that relied on split-second decisions, is a recurring theme in the annals of unconventional warfare.

> "In those moments of ambush, it wasn't just about strategy or equipment—it was about trust. Trust in your comrades, in your training, and in your own ability to make the right call in an instant," recalled Sergeant Elena,

whose unit's ambush on an enemy convoy turned the tide of a prolonged engagement. "We knew that every action, every decision, carried the weight of our mission. And when it all came together, it was like the world fell away, leaving only the pure, unfiltered reality of battle."

Their stories serve as a powerful reminder that while technology and planning are vital, the heart of warfare lies in the human capacity for courage and adaptability. These ambushes were not merely tactical ploys but expressions of human resolve—moments where individual bravery and collective ingenuity converged to redefine the battlefield.

A Tapestry of Moments and Movements

The tapestry of unorthodox battlefield tactics is woven from countless individual moments—a serendipitous turn of events, a sudden burst of audacity, a fleeting chance to strike. Each ambush and unexpected maneuver contributed to a larger narrative of resistance and innovation. The interplay between split-second decisions and their long-term strategic impact demonstrates that even the smallest tactical surprise can echo far beyond the immediate skirmish, altering the course of entire campaigns.

In the silence that follows an ambush, as enemy lines regroup and reconfigure their defenses, the true measure of success is often not visible on the battlefield but in the ripples it creates—a slowing of the enemy's advance, a fracturing of their command, a lingering sense of insecurity that can last long after the echoes of gunfire have faded.

Chapter 15: Spycraft and Innovation – Intelligence in Warfare

In the shadowy corridors of World War II, where every secret held the potential to alter the tide of battle, espionage and innovation intertwined in a high-stakes game of intelligence. Behind enemy lines and deep within clandestine networks, operatives and analysts uncovered vital information—intercepted communications, hidden documents, and covert conversations—that spurred the rapid development of experimental weaponry. This chapter explores the interplay between spycraft and technological innovation, revealing how the gathering and interpretation of secret intelligence fueled breakthroughs on the battlefield. Personal recollections from those who risked everything in the name of national security bring this hidden world into sharp focus.

The Web of Espionage

In an era defined by rapid technological advancement and ever-changing battle lines, the ability to intercept enemy communications and gather covert intelligence was as crucial as any artillery barrage. Espionage networks spanned continents—composed of double agents, radio operators, and field informants—each playing a vital role in assembling the mosaic of enemy capabilities and intentions.

- **Intercepted Communications and Signal Intelligence:**
  With the advent of sophisticated radio technology, signals intelligence (SIGINT) became a cornerstone of modern warfare. Cryptographers worked around the clock to break enemy codes, transforming garbled transmissions into actionable intelligence. Detailed intercept reports provided not only the enemy's strategic plans but also hints at the experimental projects underway in secret laboratories. These revelations spurred rapid development cycles on the home front, as engineers raced to counteract or preempt enemy innovations.
- **Coded Messages and the Art of Deception:**
  Espionage was as much an art as it was a science. Agents transmitted messages using intricate ciphers and steganographic techniques, embedding critical data within seemingly mundane reports. The interplay

between cryptographic breakthroughs and technological innovation created a feedback loop: intercepted enemy plans could lead to the development of countermeasures, which in turn necessitated more sophisticated encryption methods. Every coded message was a puzzle piece, contributing to the overall picture of enemy capabilities and the emerging landscape of experimental weaponry.

- **The Role of Human Intelligence (HUMINT):**
  Beyond the electronic signals, personal interactions played a vital role in intelligence gathering. Informants, undercover operatives, and sympathetic locals risked their lives to pass on crucial details about enemy research facilities and secret projects. Their accounts often revealed not only technical details but also the human elements—fear, ambition, and resolve—that drove innovation in enemy camps.

Accelerating Innovation Through Intelligence

The fusion of espionage and engineering was a defining characteristic of this era. Intelligence reports provided the raw data that guided experimental development on the home front. For instance, intercepted communications hinted at breakthroughs in enemy rocket technology, prompting scientists to accelerate their own research into guided missiles. In laboratories and workshops, engineers pored over translated documents, schematics, and even hand-drawn notes recovered from captured facilities.

- **Blueprints Born of Secrets:**
  Among the most significant outcomes of this exchange was the rapid evolution of experimental weapons systems. Technical blueprints, smuggled out from enemy installations, revealed innovative designs and untested ideas. Analysts and engineers collaborated, often under extreme time pressure, to adapt these concepts for their own use. The race was not merely for technological supremacy but also for the crucial advantage of knowing what the enemy might deploy next.

- **Feedback Loops Between Frontline Intelligence and Lab Innovation:**
  The continuous cycle of intelligence gathering and experimental development created a dynamic battlefield where every intercepted transmission had the potential to spark a new invention. A deciphered radio message might indicate that an enemy was testing a new type of armored vehicle or that a secret research facility was on the verge of unveiling a novel propulsion system. In response, engineers adjusted

their designs, sometimes incorporating ideas directly gleaned from the enemy's own work—always with a critical eye and a drive to outsmart the opposition.

Personal Recollections: Voices from the Shadows

The human stories behind these covert operations are as compelling as the technical innovations they inspired. The following recollections offer a glimpse into the minds and hearts of those who lived and breathed intelligence work during the war.

"Every intercepted message was a lifeline," recalled Agent Viktor, a seasoned radio operator whose covert work involved breaking enemy ciphers. "I spent countless nights in a dim room, deciphering code after code, not knowing which one would reveal the secret that could save thousands of lives. It was a constant battle against time, with every word a potential spark for a revolutionary new countermeasure."
— Agent Viktor, signals intelligence specialist

"In our lab, we often received sketches and crude diagrams of enemy weaponry—ideas that were as innovative as they were dangerous," said Dr. Helena Roth, an engineer who led a team developing experimental anti-tank systems. "There was a bittersweet irony in adapting the enemy's own innovations against them. Each breakthrough we achieved was not just a triumph of engineering but a tribute to the relentless human drive for survival and supremacy. It felt like we were racing the clock, and every decoded secret brought us one step closer to tipping the scales of war in our favor."

— Dr. Helena Roth, lead experimental weapons engineer

"I still remember the day we intercepted a message detailing the enemy's plans for a new missile system," recalled Lieutenant Samuel Price, an intelligence officer who coordinated covert operations. "It was like watching the future unfold before our eyes, and with it, the palpable fear that our adversary was always one step ahead. But that fear also fueled our determination. We knew that with every piece of intelligence, we were forging a path to counteract their innovations. It was dangerous,

exhilarating, and profoundly transformative."
— Lieutenant Samuel Price, intelligence coordinator

These firsthand accounts reveal the intense emotional landscape of intelligence work—a world where every breakthrough carried the weight of lives and the burden of responsibility. The operatives, analysts, and engineers were not merely data processors; they were guardians of hope, working in the shadows to secure a future free from tyranny.

The Enduring Legacy of Spycraft and Innovation

The legacy of World War II's intelligence efforts lives on in every modern intelligence agency and advanced weapons system. The interplay between espionage and experimental development established a new paradigm for warfare—one where the mind and the machine worked in concert to shape the course of history. The innovations born from intercepted communications and clandestine meetings not only neutralized enemy threats but also laid the foundation for the digital, networked intelligence systems we rely on today.

In the intricate dance between spycraft and innovation, every secret unlocked and every code broken was a step toward redefining warfare. The legacy of those who risked everything in the pursuit of truth serves as a powerful reminder that knowledge, when wielded with precision and courage, can be the most potent weapon of all.

Chapter 16: Field Modifications – Soldiers as On-the-Spot Inventors

In the relentless crucible of battle, where every second could mean the difference between survival and defeat, frontline troops often found themselves not only as warriors but as impromptu engineers. With supply lines stretched thin and standard-issue equipment rendered inadequate by the harsh realities of war, soldiers became the architects of their own survival. This chapter shines a light on the extraordinary ingenuity that emerged under fire—how men and women adapted their gear, modified weapons, and crafted innovative solutions on the spot, using nothing more than scrap, determination, and a desperate need to overcome overwhelming odds.

Improvisation on the Front Lines

In the midst of chaos, when the luxury of factory-made parts was a distant memory, soldiers resorted to creative modifications to keep their equipment operational. From patching up damaged vehicles with spare parts salvaged from the wreckage of battle to reconfiguring rifles for improved accuracy, every field modification was born of necessity.

- **Weapon Adaptations:**
  When a standard-issue rifle failed in the heat of combat, a soldier's quick wit often became the difference between life and death. Makeshift scopes were fashioned from broken lenses, and trigger mechanisms were fine-tuned using tools improvised from everyday objects. In some cases, entire weapons were cobbled

together by combining parts from captured enemy arms with standard gear, resulting in a hybrid that delivered unexpected performance under fire.

- **Vehicle and Equipment Repairs:** Armored vehicles and trucks, too, were not immune to the ravages of battle. In the muddy, bomb-scarred landscapes, mechanics operating alongside infantry teams would jury-rig engines using parts from disabled vehicles. Even the simplest adjustments—such as reinforcing a tire with a length of chain or patching a fuel leak with scrap metal—illustrated the relentless drive to keep moving forward, despite the odds.
- **Communication and Navigation Aids:** With radios frequently damaged or rendered inoperable by enemy fire, soldiers would often improvise communication devices. Makeshift antennae crafted from scavenged wire and tin cans became lifelines on the front, while outdated maps were annotated with fresh intelligence gleaned from the battlefield, ensuring that even in the fog of war, the team could navigate their way to safety or a decisive strike.

Diary Excerpts and Letters: Voices from the Battlefield

The true spirit of these improvised modifications is best captured in the personal accounts of those who lived through them. Soldiers' diaries and letters reveal a raw mixture of desperation, ingenuity, and hope—a testament to the human capacity to innovate even in the direst circumstances.

> "There were moments when our gear just wouldn't hold up. I remember a cold, rainy night in the trenches when my rifle jammed during a critical advance. With nothing but a pair of pliers and a scrap of metal, I managed to rig a makeshift trigger adjustment. It wasn't perfect, but it worked long enough for us to push forward. Every improvised fix felt like a small rebellion against the chaos of war."
> — Private James "Jimmy" Carter, Western Front

> "Our truck was our lifeline, but during one ambush, the engine sputtered and died. With enemy fire closing in, I had to think fast. I used a section of old piping and some rope to jury-rig a temporary repair. We limped away under cover, our hearts pounding with both fear and a wild, defiant sense of accomplishment. Every moment we survived was a victory over despair."

• • •

— Corporal Elena Morales,
Mediterranean Theater

"In a makeshift field hospital, we were
low on supplies, and even our radios
were falling apart. I fashioned a new
antenna out of wire and a tin can I
salvaged from a broken down jeep.
That tiny, clunky device became our
beacon of hope, connecting us with
headquarters when it seemed like the
world was closing in. In those dire
hours, every innovation was a lifeline."
— Sergeant Ahmed Khan, North
African Campaign

These recollections are more than historical
records—they are living testaments to the
resourcefulness that sustained countless lives.
Each improvised solution was an act of defiance, a
personal declaration that even in the midst of
relentless adversity, the human spirit could forge
new paths to survival.

The Impact of Field Modifications on Strategy

The ingenuity demonstrated by individual soldiers
had far-reaching strategic implications. Field
modifications were not isolated acts of
improvisation; they collectively contributed to a

broader evolution in military tactics. As frontline units shared their solutions—through informal networks, exchanged manuals, and whispered instructions in the dark—they built a compendium of adaptive techniques that could be replicated across units and theaters of war.

- **Rapid Adaptation and Shared Knowledge:**
  The success of a makeshift fix on one front often inspired similar improvisations elsewhere. What began as a desperate measure soon became a standardized practice. In many units, the ability to adapt and modify equipment on the fly became a valued skill, integrated into training routines and celebrated as part of the unit's identity.
- **Boosting Morale Through Ingenuity:**
  Each improvised modification served as a morale booster. Knowing that their comrades could overcome equipment failures with ingenuity instilled confidence in the soldiers, reinforcing the belief that resourcefulness was as critical to victory as firepower. This self-reliance and adaptability often turned the tide in prolonged engagements, where conventional supplies and reinforcements were uncertain.
- **Long-Term Innovations Inspired by Battlefield Ingenuity:**
  The techniques and hacks developed in the field eventually influenced post-war military

research and development. Many of the ideas born out of necessity were refined and standardized, contributing to innovations in modern weaponry and equipment design. The legacy of these field modifications is a reminder that sometimes, the most transformative ideas arise not in pristine laboratories but in the muddy, harsh realities of battle.

A Testament to the Human Spirit

In the midst of chaos, the frontline soldier emerged not only as a warrior but as an inventor—a creator whose makeshift solutions underscored the resilience of the human spirit. Every improvised repair and field modification was a small victory against an enemy determined to strip away hope. In these acts of ingenuity, the desperation of the battlefield was transformed into a powerful testament to human resourcefulness.

Through the diary entries and letters of those who experienced the harsh realities of war, we glimpse a world where every bolt tightened and every circuit soldered was an act of survival, an embodiment of defiance in the face of overwhelming odds. In the flickering light of a campfire or the dim glow of a makeshift workshop, soldiers became the unsung heroes of innovation—a legacy that continues to inspire the spirit of adaptability and courage in every generation that faces the challenge of the unknown.

Chapter 17:
Production Under Pressure – Logistics of Wartime Innovation

In the relentless crucible of global conflict, every nation faced not only the challenge of engaging the enemy but also the daunting task of sustaining a massive war effort with dwindling resources. Material shortages and manufacturing constraints

forced a radical rethinking of production methods—
sparking rapid, often improvised innovations that
kept the war machine running against all odds. This
chapter examines how logistical challenges
catalyzed a revolution in industrial production and
profiles the unsung engineers whose tireless efforts
transformed desperation into creative enterprise.

A Landscape of Scarcity and Constraint

As the conflict raged on, traditional supply lines
faltered under the strain of global demand and
enemy disruption. Factories that once produced
consumer goods were repurposed overnight into
frantic production hubs. Critical raw materials like
steel, rubber, and fuel became scarce commodities,
forcing military planners and industrial managers to
confront a harsh reality: every component had to
count.

- **Material Shortages:**
  The war exposed vulnerabilities in
  peacetime production chains. Shortages of
  essential materials meant that every spare
  ounce of metal or rubber was carefully
  rationed and, more often than not,
  redirected from civilian to military use.
  Designers and engineers were compelled to
  think in terms of "if it isn't perfect, it must be
  good enough"—a mindset that led to

innovative substitutes and resourceful reconfigurations of existing materials.

- **Manufacturing Constraints:**
  With traditional production lines operating at near-maximum capacity and enemy bombings targeting key industrial centers, the ability to mass-produce equipment became a race against time. Factories had to adapt quickly, repurposing tools and retooling assembly lines to manufacture parts that were never originally designed for warfare. It was a period when improvisation was not just a fallback option but an essential strategy for survival.

Rapid and Improvised Production Methods

In response to these constraints, engineers and factory workers alike adopted a spirit of improvisation that led to unprecedented production innovations.

- **Modular Manufacturing:**
  One key development was the introduction of modular components. Instead of waiting for a complete overhaul of manufacturing processes, engineers devised systems where parts could be produced in smaller batches and assembled quickly on the front lines. This allowed for rapid repairs and

updates to equipment, ensuring that even damaged vehicles or weapons could be returned to service with minimal downtime.

- **Adaptation of Civilian Industries:**
Many civilian factories were commandeered and reconfigured for military production. Automobile plants, for example, were transformed into assembly lines for armored vehicles and artillery parts. The ingenuity displayed in converting these facilities often meant working with outdated machinery and repurposing everyday items—like using household steel in the construction of makeshift tanks or employing surplus automotive components in aircraft engines.

- **Field Assembly and On-the-Spot Repairs:**
With supply lines constantly under threat, production wasn't confined to the factory floor. Mobile workshops and field assembly units became common sights near the front lines. Here, engineers and mechanics would combine salvaged parts with standard-issue equipment to produce critical repairs or even entirely new weapon systems. These impromptu setups were a testament to the adage that necessity is the mother of invention.

The Unsung Heroes: Engineers on the Frontlines of Innovation

Behind every improvised solution and every retooled piece of equipment stood a cadre of dedicated engineers whose names rarely made it into history books—but whose work was instrumental in sustaining the war effort.

> "Every day in the factory felt like a race against time. We had to reimagine how to use what little we had, to tweak designs that had been set in stone for decades," recalled Emil Novak, an engineer who worked in a repurposed automotive plant. "When our original blueprints couldn't be followed due to material shortages, we improvised. Each modified part was a victory—a tangible proof that even under extreme pressure, innovation could prevail."
> — Emil Novak, veteran production engineer

Their contributions were often recorded in hastily scribbled field notes and confidential memos, detailing adjustments to machinery and the creative repurposing of obsolete parts. From redesigning engine components to devising new methods of mass production, these engineers embodied resilience and resourcefulness. Their work was done under constant threat—from the risk of enemy air raids to the looming uncertainty of supply interruptions—but their resolve never wavered.

Diary Excerpts: Voices from the Industrial Front

Personal accounts from those who worked on the assembly lines provide a window into the human side of wartime production. In one diary entry, a young factory worker described the atmosphere during a particularly challenging period:

> "The sound of clanging metal was our daily anthem. Every shift was a battle against time and scarcity. I remember watching our supervisor, hands steady despite the chaos, as he retooled an entire section of the assembly line to produce spare parts for disabled tanks. In that moment, I understood that every improvised fix was more than just metal and bolts—it was hope, soldered together by sheer will."
> — Diary Entry, Eastern Front Manufacturing Unit

Another letter from a field mechanic captured the essence of these innovations on the front lines:

"We had to become our own supply chain. When our vehicle's engine failed under fire, there was no waiting for reinforcements—we fixed it on the spot using spare parts and a lot of ingenuity. It was in those moments, with sweat mingling with grease, that I realized our makeshift repairs were as crucial as any battle plan. They were the lifelines that kept us moving forward."

— Letter, North African Campaign

The Strategic Ripple Effects

The rapid, improvised production methods developed during the war had long-term implications that extended far beyond the battlefield. These innovations not only ensured that critical equipment remained operational during the height of conflict, but they also laid the groundwork for post-war industrial advancements.

- **Standardization of Modular Components:** The success of modular manufacturing during the war influenced later production strategies, emphasizing flexibility and rapid response over rigid, centralized designs. This legacy is evident in modern assembly lines and repair protocols used in various industries today.

- **Integration of Civilian and Military Technologies:**
  The seamless conversion of civilian industries into military production hubs demonstrated the potential for dual-use technologies—a concept that has since become a cornerstone of modern defense logistics.
- **Inspiration for Future Innovation:**
  The resourcefulness displayed by wartime engineers continues to inspire innovation under pressure in both military and civilian sectors. Their creative solutions remind us that constraints often serve as catalysts for breakthroughs, transforming limitations into opportunities for growth.

A Testament to Resilience and Ingenuity

In the midst of chaos, when every piece of equipment was vital and every spare part a lifeline, the ability to adapt was the key to survival. The field modifications and rapid production techniques developed under extreme conditions were more than just technical achievements—they were a profound expression of the human spirit's unyielding resolve.

The unsung engineers, mechanics, and factory workers who labored under the constant threat of disruption not only kept the war machine running but also forged a legacy of innovation that would influence generations to come. Their stories, etched into dusty memos and whispered in the quiet corridors of history, stand as a testament to the power of creative problem-solving in the face of adversity.

Chapter 18: Countermeasures – Adapting to Novel Threats

In the relentless cycle of innovation during wartime, every breakthrough in unconventional weaponry provoked an equally determined response from adversaries. As experimental devices and creative battlefield tactics emerged, opposing forces were

forced to rethink their strategies, developing
countermeasures that ranged from refined
traditional doctrines to rapid, iterative adaptations.
In this chapter, we analyze how enemies devised
counter-strategies to neutralize novel threats while
contrasting the established military doctrines with
the fluid, ever-evolving nature of wartime
innovation.

The Emergence of Adaptive Counter-Strategies

When confronted with weapons that defied
conventional expectations—from experimental
tanks and incendiary devices to improvised
firearms and covert sabotage tools—adversaries
were compelled to reassess their own tactics.
Traditional defenses, long reliant on predictable
formations and standard operating procedures,
found themselves outmatched by the unexpected.

- **Analyzing the Unorthodox:**
  Enemy commanders, upon witnessing the
  success of unconventional weapons,
  launched intensive intelligence operations to
  study their design and operational patterns.
  Detailed reconnaissance, intercepted
  communications, and captured prototypes
  provided critical data. These insights
  allowed military strategists to develop
  tailored countermeasures—from deploying

specialized anti-tank units to incorporating new forms of electronic warfare aimed at disrupting innovative guidance systems.

- **Rapid Iteration Under Pressure:** Unlike established doctrines that had evolved over decades, counter-strategies during the war were often developed in real time. Commanders implemented "trial by fire" tactics—experimenting with modified formations, revised artillery barrages, and novel camouflage techniques—to neutralize the advantages of improvised weapons. The iterative nature of these adaptations meant that countermeasures were continually refined, often in direct response to each new wave of innovation.

Traditional Doctrine vs. Iterative Innovation

The clash between time-honored military doctrines and the dynamic, iterative innovations on the battlefield created a striking contrast:

- **Rigid Structures vs. Fluid Tactics:** Traditional military doctrine emphasized large-scale maneuvers, fixed battle lines, and standardized equipment. These strategies, honed during peacetime and previous conflicts, were ill-suited to counter a foe that could improvise on the fly. In contrast, the iterative nature of wartime innovation meant that both sides were forced to adapt rapidly. The enemy's countermeasures were not static—they evolved as new unconventional weapons emerged, leading to a constant cat-and-mouse game of adaptation and response.

- **Predictability and Vulnerability:** Conventional strategies relied on predictability. Armies organized in regimented units and structured supply lines were susceptible to disruption by unexpected tactics such as ambushes, decoys, and improvised explosive devices. Recognizing this vulnerability, adversaries began to adopt more flexible, decentralized approaches, incorporating lessons learned from each engagement into their strategic playbooks. The result was a transformation from rigid, hierarchical planning to agile, responsive operations that could better withstand the shock of unconventional warfare.

Voices from the Front Lines

The human dimension of these counter-strategies reveals the high stakes and the rapid learning curve imposed by a dynamic battlefield. Personal recollections provide insight into the transformative impact of adapting to novel threats:

"We were used to fighting in well-drilled formations, our tactics refined over years of conventional combat. But when the enemy started deploying these makeshift weapons—improvised tanks and surprise ambushes—we had to rethink everything. I remember our commander calling for an emergency meeting, and within hours, we were testing new layouts, shifting to more flexible units that could react to ambushes rather than stand in rigid lines."
— Captain Robert Lang, Infantry Officer

"Every time we intercepted a transmission or captured a piece of enemy equipment, it was like adding a new piece to the puzzle. Our engineers worked round the clock, modifying our existing systems to counter the latest threat. It was a constant battle of wits, where traditional doctrine had to give way to rapid, sometimes desperate, innovation."
— Lieutenant Sofia Reyes, Signals Intelligence Analyst

These accounts underscore the profound challenge faced by military forces: adapting to a new paradigm of warfare where no plan was ever final and every innovation demanded an immediate counter-response.

The Strategic Ripple Effects

The iterative process of developing countermeasures not only neutralized individual threats but also reshaped entire strategic doctrines. As unconventional weapons forced changes in tactics, they influenced broader military planning:

- **Evolving Doctrines:**
  The persistent need to adapt led to the gradual evolution of military doctrines, where flexibility and rapid responsiveness became as critical as firepower and numbers. The lessons learned on the battlefield were integrated into training programs and strategic frameworks, laying the foundation for modern, adaptive military operations.
- **Psychological Impact on the Enemy:**
  The effectiveness of these counter-strategies also had a psychological dimension. As the enemy's unconventional weapons were increasingly neutralized, confidence in their own innovation wavered. This erosion of morale and uncertainty in enemy ranks often resulted in hesitancy and overcautious tactics—advantages that were

exploited by commanders on the opposing side.

A Battle of Minds and Machines

The struggle between innovative weaponry and adaptive countermeasures became a defining aspect of the conflict. Each side's ability to outthink and outmaneuver the other was as crucial as any technological advantage. While traditional doctrines provided a solid foundation, it was the willingness to innovate, to iterate, and to adapt that ultimately dictated success on the battlefield.

In the end, the evolution of countermeasures was a testament to the relentless ingenuity of military leaders under pressure. It was a reminder that in war, the battle is fought not only with weapons but also with ideas—and that even the most entrenched doctrines must sometimes be rewritten in the crucible of conflict.

Chapter 19: Kursk in Focus – Experimental Armor in Action

The Battle of Kursk, fought in the summer of 1943, stands as one of the most pivotal tank engagements of World War II. At Kursk, innovation and desperation collided on a vast, unforgiving battlefield where experimental armor and unorthodox tactics reshaped the art of armored warfare. In this chapter, we present a detailed case study of Kursk, examining how experimental tanks and adaptive strategies influenced the engagement. By merging technical analysis with the raw, emotional testimonies of commanders and crew members, we reveal a story of innovation under pressure—a story where every modified plate and every split-second decision altered the course of history.

The Setting: Kursk's Crucible of Innovation

Kursk was more than just a battleground—it was a laboratory for armored warfare. Facing mounting pressure to break the Soviet defenses, the German command deployed an array of experimental and modified tanks, along with novel tactical formations. On the Soviet side, hastily adapted armor and aggressive counter-tactics met these challenges head-on. In the sweltering heat and churned-up earth of the Kursk salient, every tank and crew member was part of an intricate dance between technology and human determination.

Technical Innovations on Display

Experimental Armor and Modified Tanks

At Kursk, both sides fielded vehicles that had undergone rapid modifications to address specific battlefield shortcomings:

- **German Innovations:**
  The Germans, striving to compensate for deficiencies in mobility and firepower, introduced tanks with experimental armor configurations. For example, some Tiger I units received additional frontal plating and modified turret reinforcements designed to deflect increasingly potent Soviet anti-tank rounds. Detailed schematics from the period show extra layers of hardened steel welded onto vulnerable sections, as well as revised suspension systems intended to counteract the extra weight without sacrificing maneuverability.
  Additionally, prototypes like the Ferdinand heavy tank destroyer—reborn as the Elefant after modifications—embodied the shift toward specialized, heavily armored vehicles designed for breakthrough operations.
- **Soviet Countermeasures:**
  On the Soviet side, rapid production and field modifications allowed for the integration of composite armor on Panthers and T-34s. Improvised reinforcements, often fashioned from salvaged materials and spares, were added to critical areas such as the glacis plate and turret fronts. Technical

analyses indicate that these ad hoc upgrades improved the vehicles' survivability against high-velocity penetrators, even if they could not fully match the firepower of their German counterparts.

Tactical Adaptations

The experimental nature of Kursk's armor was matched by innovative tactics:

- **Combined Arms Coordination:** Commanders on both sides increasingly relied on combined arms operations— synchronizing tanks, artillery, and infantry to maximize the impact of each assault. The Germans, for instance, employed concentrated spearheads of experimental tanks to create localized breakthroughs, expecting rapid exploitation by mechanized infantry.
- **Defensive Depth and Mobile Reserves:** The Soviets adopted a layered defense strategy, using mobile reserves to counter any sudden penetrations by enemy experimental units. These reserves were deployed in a "defense in depth" formation, where even if a unit's experimental armor was breached, subsequent layers could absorb the shock and halt the advance.

Voices from Kursk: Testimonies from the Front

The human cost and valor of Kursk are etched in the recollections of those who fought there. Their personal accounts provide a vivid window into the interplay between cutting-edge technology and the raw emotion of combat.

> "I still recall the moment when our Tiger—she was one of those experimental models—rolled into battle with that extra layer of armor. It wasn't just metal on metal; it was a statement. We knew that every modification we had fought so hard to implement was our last stand against the relentless Soviet barrage. When enemy shells clattered harmlessly off our reinforced front, there was a surge of hope mixed with a heavy burden of responsibility. It was a brief, almost surreal moment when our ingenuity seemed to hold the line."
> — Oberleutnant Klaus Richter, Tiger I crewman

> "In our unit, the T-34s had been patched and reinforced in ways you wouldn't believe. Every dent and weld told a story of desperate nights spent

in field workshops. I remember reading a letter from our driver, Dmitri, who wrote, 'Each extra bolt we fastened was like a prayer whispered in the darkness. We knew the enemy was coming, but we believed our tanks would stand firm.' That belief was our armor, as much as the metal plates covering us."
— Commissar Ivan Petrov, Soviet tank commander

"During one particularly fierce engagement, our mobile reserve had to counter a breakthrough by a formation of German experimental tanks. The chaos was indescribable—smoke, dust, and the echoing roar of engines. In that split second of decision-making, our instincts took over. We moved quickly, repositioning our artillery and coordinating with infantry. It wasn't just tactics; it was the culmination of every lesson learned in the field. We were fighting for every inch of ground, every modified plate, every heartbeat."
— Lieutenant Sergei Mikhailov, Soviet infantry officer

The Strategic Ripple Effect

• • •

The innovations and countermeasures displayed at Kursk did more than determine the outcome of a single battle—they reshaped the doctrines of armored warfare:

- **Iterative Learning on the Battlefield:**
  The rapid modifications and experimental deployments forced both sides to continuously adapt. What began as a tentative foray into enhanced armor became a catalyst for broader industrial and tactical reforms. Lessons from Kursk informed post-war designs, where modularity and rapid field modifications became standard.
- **Psychological Impact:**
  The sight of heavily modified tanks on both sides, their armor pockmarked with the scars of battle yet seemingly impervious to incoming fire, had a profound psychological effect. For German crews, every additional reinforcement was a lifeline—a testament to their relentless pursuit of perfection. For Soviet troops, witnessing the adaptability of their own equipment bolstered their resolve, proving that innovation could turn the tide even when conventional strength faltered.
- **Doctrine Transformation:**
  The Battle of Kursk underscored that the future of armored warfare lay not in static designs but in the dynamic interplay between technology and battlefield realities. This realization spurred a shift away from

rigid, pre-war doctrines toward flexible, responsive strategies that could evolve in real time—a legacy that endures in modern military planning.

Kursk: A Crucible of Courage and Innovation

Kursk remains a powerful reminder that the fusion of experimental technology and human determination can redefine the course of history. In the heat of battle, every modified tank, every tactical adjustment, and every act of bravery was a testament to the unyielding spirit of those who dared to innovate under fire.

The legacy of Kursk is not measured solely in the numbers of tanks lost or won, but in the transformative power of human ingenuity—a force that, even amid the carnage, illuminated a path toward a future where adaptability and courage stand as the true armaments of war.

Chapter 20: Rocket Revolution – The V-1 and V-2 Legacy

Few innovations in modern warfare have left as indelible a mark as the birth of guided missiles. In World War II, the development of the V-1 and V-2 rockets signaled a seismic shift in military technology, ushering in the era of rocket propulsion and guided munitions. This chapter offers an in-depth exploration of the design, deployment, and tactical impact of these pioneering systems, weaving together technical analysis with firsthand accounts from engineers and intelligence analysts who witnessed their revolutionary impact firsthand.

The Genesis of Rocketry

The path to the V-1 and V-2 rockets was paved by decades of theoretical research and experimental trials. Early rocketry—once the province of isolated visionaries—found its moment under the crucible of global conflict. With traditional artillery and aircraft reaching their limits, both the Allies and the Axis sought weapons that could deliver precision strikes over vast distances.

- **The V-1 "Buzz Bomb":**
  The V-1 was conceived as a relatively simple pulsejet-powered missile. Its design prioritized mass production and rapid deployment. Technical schematics reveal an aerodynamic body with a fixed wing assembly, a rudimentary guidance system based on preset altitudes and speeds, and a pulsejet engine that produced the distinctive buzzing sound. The V-1's design was not flawless—it was vulnerable to countermeasures—but it served as a crucial stepping stone toward more advanced systems.

- **The V-2 "Wunderwaffe":**
  In contrast, the V-2 was a marvel of engineering—a liquid-fueled, supersonic ballistic missile that broke new ground in both performance and destructive power. Detailed technical documents show that the V-2 incorporated advanced features such as gyroscopic stabilization, an innovative propulsion system capable of sustaining high-altitude flight, and a guidance mechanism that, while primitive by modern standards, was revolutionary for its time. The V-2's ability to travel at speeds exceeding 3,500 km/h rendered conventional anti-air defenses virtually useless.

From Blueprint to Battlefield

The transition from laboratory prototypes to operational weapons involved an extraordinary leap in both engineering and logistics. Engineers worked under extreme pressure, often in clandestine facilities, to refine these designs for mass production and combat use.

- **Engineering Challenges:**
  For the V-1, engineers had to perfect the pulsejet engine—a task that involved balancing fuel efficiency with sufficient thrust. Modifications to the engine casing

and the integration of simple guidance fins were pivotal. In contrast, the V-2 required innovations in liquid fuel handling and high-temperature materials. Detailed blueprints show precise calculations for combustion chamber geometry, cooling systems, and the integration of gyroscopic stabilizers that would later influence modern missile design.

"Every time we tested a component of the V-2, it felt like we were peering into the future of warfare," recalled Dr. Erich Müller, a lead engineer in one of the secret development units. "The technical hurdles were immense, but each breakthrough validated our belief that we were on the cusp of a revolution."

- **Mass Production Under Duress:**
  With the war intensifying, production facilities were repurposed overnight. Factories once devoted to civilian goods were transformed into high-speed assembly lines for rocket components. Engineers devised modular production techniques, allowing for rapid assembly even when supplies were constrained. This rapid production cycle was critical, as both the V-1 and V-2 were deployed in significant numbers, each representing a new tool in the arsenal of modern warfare.

Tactical Impact and Battlefield Legacy

The introduction of guided missiles fundamentally altered strategic calculations on both sides of the conflict. While the V-1's relatively unsophisticated guidance allowed for countermeasures to be developed, its terror and unpredictability had a profound psychological effect on civilian populations and military planners alike. The V-2, however, changed the game entirely.

- **Psychological Warfare:**
  The V-1, often heard before it was seen, instilled fear and anxiety. Its droning buzz became synonymous with impending doom. Despite its limitations, the psychological impact of the V-1 forced Allied air defenses into overdrive, diverting precious resources. The V-2's supersonic speed and devastating impact further amplified this effect. Commanders noted that the sudden, unstoppable nature of the V-2 attacks disrupted not only enemy formations but also their strategic planning.

  "When the first V-2 hit, it was like witnessing a force of nature—an unstoppable surge that left us scrambling for cover and answers," recalled Lieutenant Samuel Price, an intelligence analyst who tracked missile deployments. "It wasn't just a weapon; it was a declaration that the rules of war were being rewritten before our eyes."

- **Strategic Shifts:**
  The deployment of these rockets forced military strategists to reconsider the very nature of defense. Traditional anti-aircraft guns and fighter intercepts were rendered largely ineffective against the V-2's high-altitude trajectory and supersonic velocity. This led to a reallocation of resources toward new defensive technologies, such as early-warning radar systems and advanced missile countermeasures—a legacy that echoes in the modern age of integrated air defense.

Voices from the Vanguard

The story of the V-1 and V-2 is as much about the men and women behind the technology as it is about the machines themselves. Personal recollections from engineers and intelligence operatives offer a window into the extraordinary mix of triumph and trepidation that defined this era.

"Working on the V-2 was both exhilarating and harrowing," reflected Dr. Müller. "Every successful test fired a surge of adrenaline, knowing that our work could shift the balance of the war. Yet, there was always a shadow of doubt—wondering if we were creating a tool for destruction that we might one day regret. It was a constant moral and technical tightrope." — Dr. Erich Müller, Lead V-2 Engineer

"From an intelligence perspective, intercepting messages about V-1 launch sites was a game-changer," added Agent Viktor, a signals intelligence specialist. "We would work day and night deciphering enemy codes, and each decoded message provided a glimpse into a new frontier of warfare. The more we learned, the more we realized that these rockets were not just weapons—they were harbingers of a new era." — Agent Viktor, Signals Intelligence Specialist

"The night we saw our first V-1 over the city, I felt an unshakeable chill," recalled Captain Ingrid Weber, a commander responsible for coordinating air defenses. "It was as if a new, invisible enemy had taken to the skies. Every whir of its engine was a reminder of how swiftly technology was changing the battlefield—and how

desperately we had to adapt." —
Captain Ingrid Weber, Air Defense
Commander

The Enduring Legacy of Rocketry

The innovations embodied in the V-1 and V-2 rockets laid the groundwork for the future of missile technology. The rapid pace of their development, the lessons learned in their deployment, and the psychological impact they had on both enemy and ally reshaped military doctrine in ways that persist to this day. Their legacy is a testament to the power of human ingenuity, even when it is harnessed for destruction.

In the annals of military history, the rocket revolution stands as a pivotal chapter—a moment when the convergence of scientific ambition, desperate necessity, and the relentless drive to innovate propelled humanity into a new era of warfare. The personal accounts and technical breakthroughs of the V-1 and V-2 not only mark a turning point in the art of combat but also serve as enduring reminders of the profound and sometimes ambivalent legacy of technological progress.

Chapter 21: Unsung Innovators – The Engineers Behind the Scenes

Behind every headline of battlefield heroics and strategic triumphs, there exists a quieter, equally crucial narrative: the story of the engineers whose inventive contributions turned the tide of war. In this chapter, we shine a light on the lesser-known figures—those whose brilliant ideas, precise calculations, and relentless determination provided the technical backbone of wartime success. Their innovations, often crafted in dimly lit workshops or crowded factory floors, were not merely mechanical marvels; they were human triumphs in the face of adversity.

The Hidden Architects of Innovation

In a world where the roar of cannons and the whir of aircraft dominated the public eye, the detailed work of engineers was often relegated to the background. Yet, in every modified tank, every retooled weapon system, and every improvised production method, the fingerprints of unsung innovators can be found. These men and women, working in secrecy and under extreme pressure, devised solutions that allowed armies to adapt quickly and efficiently to an ever-changing battlefield.

Alexei Kuznetsov – The Tactician of T-34 Upgrades

Alexei Kuznetsov, a modest engineer stationed at a remote Soviet factory, was instrumental in developing field modifications for the T-34. Working with a small team under constant threat of enemy air raids, Kuznetsov devised a method to reinforce the T-34's glacis plate using locally sourced composite materials. His solution, which involved layering scrap metal with experimental heat-resistant alloys, significantly increased the tank's survivability during direct assaults.

> "I never imagined that a few hours in a makeshift workshop, surrounded by cold metal and fading blueprints, could change the fate of our battalions," Alexei recalled in a rare interview. "Every weld, every modification, was driven by the hope that our humble work might give our soldiers a fighting chance."

Rosa Martinez – The Pioneer of Rapid Field Repairs

Halfway across the continent, in a repurposed automotive plant in the Mediterranean theater, Rosa Martinez led a team of technicians who specialized in rapid field repairs. Known for her resourcefulness, Rosa transformed broken-down engines and damaged chassis into viable, battle-ready machines. By innovating a modular repair system—using interchangeable parts and streamlined procedures—she not only reduced downtime but also inspired a generation of field mechanics to see potential where others saw only scrap.

"Repairing a tank in the midst of battle isn't just about fixing a machine—it's about restoring hope," Rosa wrote in a personal diary entry. "Every bolt tightened and every piece replaced was a silent promise to our comrades: that no matter how dire the situation, we would find a way to keep moving forward."

John Robertson – The Quiet Genius of Logistics Engineering

In the chaotic environs of a commandeered factory in war-torn Britain, John Robertson worked tirelessly to retool production lines for military use. With supplies scarce and time in short order, John developed an innovative system that allowed for the rapid assembly of critical components for anti-aircraft artillery. His methods, characterized by a series of simple yet effective assembly techniques, minimized waste and maximized output. Though his work was never celebrated on the front pages, his designs ensured that vital equipment reached the frontline when it was needed most.

"Every day I felt the weight of responsibility—knowing that my small contributions could mean the difference between a well-fortified position and a catastrophic failure," John later reflected in a handwritten letter archived in a family collection. "It was about precision, yes, but also about the quiet satisfaction of knowing that ingenuity, in its purest form, can overcome even the harshest limitations."

Humanizing the Technical Narrative

These personal sketches and recollections reveal that behind every technical schematic lies a human story of struggle, innovation, and resilience. The unsung engineers of World War II were not distant figures of abstract brilliance; they were individuals who faced immense personal risks and moral dilemmas, working under conditions that demanded both intellectual rigor and unwavering courage.

- **The Pressure of Innovation:** Working under constant threat—from enemy bombings to the relentless pressure of production quotas—these engineers often wrote in their diaries about the tension between duty and exhaustion. Their notes, filled with technical details interspersed with moments of quiet introspection, show a humanity that persisted despite the overwhelming odds.
- **Moments of Triumph and Reflection:** In the glow of a flickering workshop light, as

a prototype finally roared to life or a field modification proved its worth on the battlefield, there was often a shared, silent celebration. These moments, though fleeting, were imbued with the knowledge that every small success was a victory over the chaos of war.

- **Legacy Beyond the Battlefield:** The innovations crafted by these unsung heroes laid the groundwork for post-war technological advancements. Their methods of rapid field repairs, modular production techniques, and adaptive design have transcended their wartime origins, continuing to inspire engineers in both military and civilian sectors today.

The Enduring Spirit of the Innovators

In chronicling the contributions of Alexei, Rosa, John, and countless others, we uncover a fundamental truth: that the ingenuity of the human spirit is often most visible in moments of crisis. Their technical achievements were not isolated acts of mechanical genius but expressions of a deeper, resilient determination to defy fate. As much as they reengineered tanks, radios, and production lines, they also redefined the very concept of innovation under pressure.

Their stories, etched in faded blueprints, scribbled diary entries, and whispered recollections, remind us that even in the darkest times, there exists a light—a spark of creativity that can transform despair into progress. The unsung innovators of World War II are a testament to the power of human resilience, proving that when the stakes are highest, ordinary people can achieve extraordinary feats.

Chapter 22: Airborne Evolution – Paratroopers and Tactical Shifts

The art of warfare was transformed when men and women began to descend from the skies, their freefall marking the birth of a new era in military strategy. Airborne operations evolved from daring experiments into a decisive force that reshaped battlefields and redefined what was possible in modern combat. This chapter traces that evolution—from the pioneering innovations in parachute design and transport aircraft to the strategic brilliance that allowed paratroopers to seize the initiative. Vivid sensory depictions of the drop, the rush of air and adrenaline, and the thunderous impact of landing are interwoven with strategic insights from field commanders, revealing a world where split-second decisions in the sky had far-reaching consequences on the ground.

The Genesis of Airborne Warfare

Long before paratroopers became a common sight in battle, visionaries and military strategists dared to imagine a force that could bypass entrenched enemy lines entirely. The concept was radical: deploy soldiers from aircraft behind enemy defenses, striking deep into the heart of the adversary's strongholds. Early experimental jumps demonstrated that the element of surprise, combined with rapid mobility, could turn the tide of battle.

Innovations in aircraft design were crucial. Modified bombers, originally built for strategic bombing, were refitted to carry paratroopers, while new models emerged with reinforced floors and open doors to facilitate mass drops. At the same time, advancements in parachute technology—such as steerable canopies and more reliable ripcord systems—gave jumpers the ability to control their descent and aim for designated drop zones. These technical breakthroughs, born out of necessity and honed through trial and error, laid the foundation for airborne operations that could be executed with precision and impact.

The Sensory Experience of the Freefall

For those who leaped from the aircraft, the experience was a rush of adrenaline and raw emotion. The roar of the engines, the vibration of the fuselage, and the sudden burst of cold wind as the door swung open created a sensory assault that was both terrifying and exhilarating.

> "When the door opened and I stepped into the void, it was like plunging into a vortex of wind and fear. The deafening roar of the aircraft faded, replaced by a rush of cold air that sent shivers down my spine. In that heart-stopping moment, the only thing I could feel was the weightlessness of freedom—and the burden of what lay ahead."
> — Captain David Mercer, veteran paratrooper

As jumpers tumbled through the sky, the world below transformed into a patchwork of fields, forests, and enemy fortifications. The sensation of freefall was punctuated by the sudden, jarring deployment of the parachute—a canopy that, once fully open, slowed the descent and allowed for a brief, surreal moment of control. The soft rustle of the canopy, the scent of high-altitude cold, and the distant, muffled sounds of the battlefield converged into an experience that would be etched in memory forever.

Tactical Shifts and Strategic Impact

The integration of airborne operations into military doctrine forced a dramatic reevaluation of traditional battle strategies. Field commanders quickly recognized that the ability to drop troops behind enemy lines could disrupt conventional defensive formations and create chaos in the enemy's rear areas.

- **Breaking Through Defensive Lines:** Airborne forces had the unique advantage of bypassing the heavily fortified front, allowing them to strike at critical supply lines, communication centers, and command hubs. This capability compelled enemy commanders to rethink their static defenses. "When paratroopers hit, it was like a bolt of lightning tearing through a calm sky," recalled General Harold Westwood, a senior strategist. "Our enemy was forced to divert resources to guard against an invisible threat, and that disruption alone could tilt the balance of a campaign."

- **Rapid Deployment and Flexibility:**
The speed with which airborne units could be inserted, seize key terrain, and then link up with advancing ground forces was a game-changer. These operations, often executed under the cover of darkness or in adverse weather conditions, required seamless coordination between pilots, jumpers, and ground commanders. The element of surprise—combined with the inherent mobility of airborne troops— created opportunities for rapid exploitation, forcing adversaries to react on multiple fronts simultaneously.

- **Psychological Warfare from Above:**
Beyond their physical impact, airborne operations carried a significant psychological weight. The sudden appearance of paratroopers in the enemy's rear instilled a sense of vulnerability and uncertainty. Troops who had been prepared for frontal assaults now had to contend with attacks from unseen angles. "There's a distinct terror in knowing that your enemy can strike from the skies at any moment," explained Lieutenant Colonel Maria

Sanchez, a strategic operations planner. "It creates an atmosphere of constant vigilance that erodes morale and disrupts command structures."

Case Studies: Airborne Operations in Action

Several landmark operations illustrate the transformative power of airborne tactics:

- **Operation Market Garden:**
  One of the most ambitious airborne operations in history, Operation Market Garden aimed to capture a series of key bridges in the Netherlands. Although the operation ultimately fell short of its objectives, the initial drops demonstrated the potential of paratroopers to secure strategic positions quickly. The operation forced enemy forces to reallocate defensive resources, even as the paratroopers faced the harsh realities of prolonged isolation behind enemy lines.
- **Eastern Front Airborne Drops:**
  On the vast, frozen expanses of the Eastern Front, airborne operations were executed under brutal conditions. Paratroopers faced not only enemy fire but also the severe challenges of extreme cold and unpredictable weather. These operations,

marked by moments of both chaos and precision, underscored the resilience and adaptability of airborne troops. The lessons learned in these harsh environments helped refine airborne tactics for future conflicts.

The Duality of Airborne Warfare

Airborne operations encapsulated a powerful duality: the juxtaposition of exhilaration and terror, freedom and vulnerability. For the paratroopers, every jump was a leap of faith—a risk that could either secure a decisive victory or end in catastrophic loss. The split-second decisions made during freefall and the subsequent coordination on the ground required nerves of steel and an unwavering commitment to the mission.

> "Every jump was a gamble," reflected Captain Mercer. "The freefall was a moment of pure, unfiltered adrenaline, where the only constant was the pounding of your heart and the knowledge that there was no turning back. But when you landed and saw the impact you had made—a bridge captured, a supply line cut—it was a validation of every risk, every ounce of courage we mustered."

— Captain David Mercer, veteran
paratrooper

The evolution of airborne operations not only
revolutionized how battles were fought but also
reshaped military strategy for generations to come.
The innovations in aircraft modification, parachute
technology, and tactical coordination continue to
underpin modern rapid deployment forces and
special operations. The legacy of these airborne
pioneers is a testament to the transformative power
of taking risks—both technological and human—to
achieve objectives that once seemed impossible.

A Lasting Legacy

Today, the principles of airborne warfare remain a
critical component of military strategy around the
world. The lessons learned from those early, daring
leaps into the unknown continue to inspire new
generations of soldiers, pilots, and strategists. In
every modern air assault and every coordinated
rapid deployment, echoes of that revolutionary
evolution can be heard—a constant reminder that
the courage to defy gravity is matched only by the
will to overcome any obstacle.

In the evolving landscape of warfare, the airborne
revolution stands as a beacon of human ingenuity
and valor. As we look to the future, the daring spirit
of those who jumped into the void—where every
descent was both an act of defiance and a

• • •

declaration of hope—remains an enduring inspiration for all who dare to challenge the boundaries of possibility.

Chapter 23: Sea Change – Redefining Naval Strategy

The vast, unpredictable ocean has long been a theater of both brute force and subtle genius. During World War II, the balance of power at sea was dramatically shifted by unorthodox vessel designs and innovative tactics that defied traditional naval doctrine. In this chapter, we explore key naval engagements where creative engineering and daring strategies transformed maritime conflict. Detailed descriptions capture the deafening roar of engines, the creak of timbers under relentless waves, and the raw emotions of sailors navigating the chaos of battle.

Unconventional Vessel Designs

Traditional warships—grand battleships and stalwart cruisers—had dominated naval warfare for generations. Yet, as the conflict intensified, both adversaries began experimenting with vessel designs that emphasized stealth, speed, and agility over sheer size.

- **Streamlined U-Boats and Submersible Innovations:**
  German U-boats evolved dramatically during the war. By incorporating improved hull designs and quieter propulsion systems, these submarines could slip silently beneath the ocean's surface. The low, sleek profile of the later models was a stark contrast to earlier, bulkier designs. Inside, cramped quarters were filled with constant vibrations and the low hum of diesel engines—a continuous reminder of the dangerous, covert world beneath the waves.

- **Modified Patrol Craft and Fast Attack Boats:**
  On the surface, smaller, agile vessels were adapted for hit-and-run tactics. These fast attack boats, often modified from civilian fishing trawlers or merchant ships, featured reinforced hulls and concealed armaments. Their design allowed them to dart in and out of enemy convoys, delivering surprise attacks and vanishing before a counterstrike could be mounted. The sight of these nimble crafts slicing through turbulent seas, their engines singing a high-pitched, insistent tune, was both awe-inspiring and terrifying.
- **Hybrid Designs and Experimental Concepts:**
  Some navies experimented with hybrid vessels that combined the attributes of submarines and surface ships. These "submersible cruisers" could operate on the surface in calm conditions and dive beneath enemy radar when danger loomed. Their innovative design was marked by retractable masts, variable ballast systems, and cutting-edge communication arrays— each detail a product of meticulous engineering under pressure.

Innovative Tactics at Sea

Unorthodox vessel designs went hand in hand with novel tactics that challenged centuries-old maritime doctrines. Commanders learned that the key to naval supremacy was no longer merely firepower or armor, but the ability to adapt and exploit the enemy's vulnerabilities.

- **Ambush and Hit-and-Run Strategies:** Naval engagements increasingly featured ambush tactics reminiscent of guerrilla warfare. Smaller, fast-moving vessels were deployed to intercept and disrupt enemy convoys. These surprise attacks relied on impeccable timing and a deep understanding of the ocean's hidden lanes. The shock of a sudden assault—when enemy ships were caught off guard by a barrage of torpedoes or machine-gun fire— was amplified by the silence that often followed the initial chaos, leaving a void filled with uncertainty and dread.
- **Decoys and Electronic Deception:** In a bid to confuse enemy radar and sonar, navies began using decoy vessels and jamming techniques. Inflatable rafts painted to resemble full-sized warships were deployed as moving targets, while specialized electronic countermeasures created ghost signals on enemy screens. These tactics forced adversaries to second-guess their intelligence, turning the very

ocean into a labyrinth of false leads and red herrings.

- **Coordinated Flotilla Maneuvers:**
  Beyond individual skirmishes, large-scale naval battles saw the rise of coordinated flotilla tactics. Commanders orchestrated complex maneuvers where groups of vessels, including reinvigorated destroyers, modified patrol boats, and stealthy submarines, worked in concert to encircle and overwhelm enemy formations. The ebb and flow of these battles, where every turn of the ship could determine victory or defeat, was a testament to the evolving nature of maritime strategy.

The Sensory World of Maritime Conflict

The ocean is a realm of extremes—a vast stage where every sound, sight, and sensation is magnified in moments of crisis.

- **The Roar of Engines and the Crash of Waves:**
  Amid the chaos of battle, the incessant drone of ship engines blends with the rhythmic crash of relentless waves. The soundscape is punctuated by the distant boom of explosions, the high-pitched whine of torpedoes slicing through water, and the

eerie silence that follows a successful ambush. Each sound conveys a story: the steadfast determination of a crew, the sudden terror of an unexpected attack, or the resolute calm that descends just before a coordinated strike.

- **Visual Spectacles on the High Seas:**
At sea, the visual drama is equally compelling. Imagine the sight of sleek vessels darting through choppy waters, their silhouettes outlined against a blood-red sunset. In the midst of battle, plumes of black smoke rise from damaged ships, while searchlights cut through the night like beams of pure determination. The interplay of light and shadow on the rolling sea creates a canvas that is as beautiful as it is brutal.

- **The Emotional Weight of Maritime Warfare:**
The life of a sailor during these turbulent times was marked by moments of both intense fear and profound camaraderie. The close quarters of a ship, the shared anxieties during enemy engagements, and the fleeting moments of triumph when innovative tactics turned the tide of battle left an indelible mark on those who served. Personal recollections speak of the bitter cold of long nights at sea, the sweat and salt of close-quarters combat, and the

unspoken bond forged among those who faced the ocean's fury together.

Voices from the Deep

Personal testimonies from commanders and crew members bring this world to life, offering glimpses into the human experience behind the technical marvels.

"I'll never forget the day our decoy flotilla misdirected an entire enemy convoy. The calm before the storm was palpable—we could almost hear our hearts beating in unison with the lapping of waves. Then, in a matter of moments, our fast attack boats descended like sharks, and the chaos that ensued was unlike anything I'd ever witnessed."
— Commander Harold Jenkins, Naval Operations

"Every time I stood on the deck and saw our modified patrol craft slip silently through the mist, I felt a mixture of awe and trepidation. The ocean was our battlefield, and its unpredictable nature made every encounter a test of both skill and nerve. There was beauty in the chaos—a fleeting, almost surreal moment when strategy and nature

converged."
— Lieutenant Sarah Monroe, Patrol
Boat Captain

Strategic Impact and the Future of Naval Warfare

The unorthodox vessel designs and innovative tactics deployed during these naval engagements did more than secure temporary victories; they redefined the future of maritime strategy. The success of decoy operations, stealthy submarine incursions, and coordinated flotilla maneuvers influenced post-war naval doctrines and the development of modern warships.

- **Evolving Doctrine:**
  The lessons learned at sea—where rapid adaptation and creative tactics often outpaced raw firepower—paved the way for the flexible, technology-driven strategies that characterize modern navies. Today's aircraft carriers, stealth destroyers, and advanced submarines owe a debt to the pioneers of unorthodox warfare who proved that the ocean's depths could be just as dynamic as its surface.
- **A Legacy of Innovation:**
  The spirit of maritime innovation endures in every new design and tactical concept. As technology continues to evolve, the

principles forged in the heat of naval conflict remain a guiding light, reminding us that the true power of naval strategy lies not just in the might of a ship, but in the ingenuity of those who dare to redefine what is possible.

Chapter 24:
Technology Meets Tactics – The Strategic Impact of Innovation

In the vast, ever-shifting theater of war, every technological breakthrough rippled far beyond the confines of its design. Groundbreaking machinery—whether it was an experimental tank, a guided missile, or a stealth aircraft—did not simply add firepower to the battlefield; it reshaped strategic decision-making and redefined how battles were won or lost. In this chapter, we explore how innovative technologies influenced military strategy and battlefield outcomes while reflecting on the dynamic interplay between technological progress and the indomitable spirit of human ingenuity.

Shaping Strategy with Groundbreaking Machinery

Modern warfare evolved as armies embraced machines that once existed only in blueprints and laboratories. These advancements forced military leaders to reconsider traditional doctrines and adapt their strategies in real time:

- **Decisive Edge on the Battlefield:** New machinery, such as the experimental tanks with advanced armor configurations or guided missiles that rendered anti-air defenses obsolete, provided commanders with a critical edge. The ability to strike swiftly and unpredictably altered long-established battle plans. Commanders no longer relied solely on massed infantry or artillery barrages—instead, they integrated these innovations into fast-paced, coordinated maneuvers that exploited enemy vulnerabilities.

- **Integration of Multi-Domain Operations:**
  Ground, air, and naval forces increasingly
  operated as interdependent components of
  a larger, unified strategy. For instance, the
  rapid deployment of airborne forces
  combined with precision-guided munitions
  created a synergy that was greater than the
  sum of its parts. The introduction of radar,
  improved communications, and electronic
  countermeasures further allowed strategic
  commands to monitor and adapt to enemy
  movements in real time. This integration
  was essential in planning large-scale
  offensives where timing and coordination
  could mean the difference between victory
  and defeat.
- **The Feedback Loop of Innovation:**
  Each new technology prompted both sides
  to innovate further. When one side unveiled
  a machine that disrupted enemy formations
  or rendered conventional defenses
  ineffective, adversaries scrambled to
  develop countermeasures. This relentless
  cycle pushed the boundaries of what was
  technologically possible, with every
  innovation inciting a strategic reevaluation.
  Battlefield outcomes began to hinge as
  much on the speed of technological
  adaptation as on traditional combat
  prowess.

The Interplay Between Technology and Human Ingenuity

While the machinery of war was increasingly sophisticated, its true power lay in the human capacity to adapt, improvise, and harness these tools to their fullest potential. The relationship between technology and human ingenuity was complex, marked by both awe and ethical ambivalence:

- **Creative Adaptation in the Face of Constraints:**
  Engineers and soldiers alike worked tirelessly to overcome the limitations of available resources. Improvised modifications, as seen in field repairs and on-the-spot adaptations, underscored that even the most advanced technology required human insight to be effective. Every new machine was not just a triumph of engineering—it was a testament to the resolve and creativity of those who deployed it in the face of insurmountable odds.
- **Balancing Innovation and Ethics:**
  With every leap in technology came profound questions about its use. The development of weapons capable of unprecedented destruction forced military

leaders and engineers to confront the moral implications of their work. Amid the triumph of innovation was a persistent tension: the same ingenuity that enabled technological breakthroughs also carried the potential for catastrophic consequences. This delicate balance between progress and responsibility remains a timeless dilemma in the annals of military history.

- **Human Stories Behind the Machines:** Personal recollections from field commanders, engineers, and soldiers reveal that technological advancements were more than just tools—they were extensions of human will. A general's decisive orders to integrate a new missile system, the hushed conversations of engineers laboring late into the night to perfect a design, or a soldier's quiet pride in operating a retooled weapon all highlight the human element driving innovation. These voices remind us that while machines can change the face of warfare, it is human ingenuity, courage, and adaptability that ultimately shape its outcome.

Reflections on the Legacy of Innovation

The strategic impact of technological progress during World War II has left an enduring legacy on modern military doctrine. Today's armed forces, with their advanced systems and integrated digital networks, owe much to the iterative process of innovation that defined the war. Yet, the lessons extend beyond mere tactics and technology; they serve as a reminder that innovation is inherently a human endeavor—a process fueled by both brilliant minds and the relentless desire to overcome adversity.

As we look back on the transformative period when technology met tactics on the battlefield, we see that every groundbreaking machine was both a product of its time and a harbinger of the future. The interplay between technological progress and human ingenuity not only redefined strategic decision-making but also demonstrated that the spirit of innovation can thrive even in the darkest hours of conflict.

In the end, the true measure of military success was not found solely in the machines that roared into battle, but in the creative strategies and adaptive minds that wielded them. It is this symbiosis—the merging of steel and spirit, precision and passion—that continues to drive the evolution of warfare, reminding us that while technology may provide the tools, it is human ingenuity that ultimately determines the course of history.

Chapter 25: Legacy and Reflection – The Enduring Impact of Curiosity

As the tumult of World War II recedes into history, the innovations born from that period continue to shape our world—both on the battlefield and beyond. The breakthroughs forged in a crucible of desperation and ingenuity have left a legacy that extends far into modern military thought. In this final chapter, we examine how a spirit of relentless curiosity and adaptation not only redefined warfare in its time but also laid the groundwork for today's strategic doctrines and technological advancements. We reflect on the profound human, ethical, and societal costs of wartime innovation, inviting readers to ponder the universal drive to adapt and overcome.

Bridging Past and Present

The extraordinary achievements of wartime innovation did more than determine the outcome of battles; they transformed the very fabric of military strategy. The modular designs, rapid production techniques, and unconventional tactics developed under fire became blueprints for modern warfare. Today's advanced communication networks, precision-guided munitions, and agile combat systems trace their origins to the experiments and improvised solutions that emerged during World War II.

Military academies and strategic think tanks continue to study these early innovations as case studies in adaptability. For instance, the iterative process by which engineers refined experimental tanks, rockets, and aircraft has evolved into today's agile development cycles in defense research. Modern commanders rely on principles of flexibility and rapid response—tenets that were honed in the crucible of war—to address emerging threats in an increasingly unpredictable global landscape.

The evolution from static, rigid doctrines to fluid, integrated strategies exemplifies the lasting impact of wartime innovation. Just as the fusion of ground, air, and naval operations redefined combat during the war, contemporary multi-domain operations continue to draw from that same legacy, blurring the lines between different realms of warfare and harnessing the collective power of technology and human ingenuity.

The Human Cost of Innovation

Yet, behind every technological marvel lies a story of sacrifice. Wartime innovation came at an enormous human cost. In the rush to develop new weapons and tactics, countless lives were irrevocably changed—lost or forever scarred by the destructive power they helped unleash. The engineers who labored in dim, bombed-out factories and the soldiers who risked everything to deploy these innovations did so under conditions of immense pressure and moral ambiguity.

Diaries, letters, and personal accounts reveal a poignant duality: a mixture of pride in technological achievement and profound sorrow for the lives disrupted or ended by these breakthroughs. Each new machine, each novel tactic, was both a symbol of human progress and a reminder of the heavy toll exacted by war. The ethical dilemmas faced by scientists and military leaders continue to resonate, challenging us to reflect on how we balance the pursuit of innovation with the imperative to preserve human life.

> "Every breakthrough felt like a double-edged sword," wrote one engineer in a long-forgotten journal entry. "We were building the future, but with every prototype, I could not shake the thought that our work would be measured in human lives. The tension between progress and its cost was our constant companion."
> — Anonymous Engineer

Ethical Quandaries and the Dual Legacy

The legacy of wartime innovation is steeped in ethical complexities. On one hand, the rapid development of groundbreaking technology saved lives by ending conflicts more swiftly and deterring further aggression. On the other, these same technologies ushered in an era of unprecedented destruction, raising questions about the moral responsibility of inventors and strategists.

This duality forces us to confront uncomfortable questions: How do we measure the value of progress when it comes at such a high human price? Can the pursuit of technological superiority ever be justified if it perpetuates cycles of violence? The innovations of World War II compel us to consider not only the capabilities they bestowed upon nations but also the enduring ethical challenges they pose—a conversation that remains as relevant today as it was then.

Inspiration for Future Endeavors

In examining the legacy of wartime innovation, we also find a wellspring of inspiration. The same spirit of curiosity and resilience that propelled engineers to overcome resource shortages, adapt to enemy strategies, and repurpose every scrap of metal in the pursuit of victory continues to inspire modern research and development. Today's breakthroughs in cyber warfare, unmanned systems, and artificial intelligence are built upon the foundation laid by those who dared to challenge convention in the face of overwhelming adversity.

The innovative methodologies refined during the war have transcended the battlefield, influencing industries and academic research worldwide. From modular design principles to rapid prototyping and decentralized production, the lessons learned under fire have been repurposed to drive progress in medicine, technology, and engineering. This enduring legacy reminds us that adversity often serves as the catalyst for breakthroughs that can transform society.

Pondering Our Collective Future

As we reflect on the enduring impact of wartime innovation, it is essential to recognize that the drive to adapt and overcome is a universal human trait. The same curiosity that led to the creation of experimental tanks, guided missiles, and improvised weapons under dire circumstances continues to propel humanity forward in times of peace and conflict alike.

Modern military thought, as well as broader technological and societal progress, is built upon a foundation of iterative learning, ethical introspection, and relentless innovation. However, as we chart our path into an uncertain future, we must remain mindful of the lessons of the past. The balance between technological advancement and its moral implications is delicate and requires constant vigilance. In our pursuit of new frontiers— whether in the realms of space exploration, cyber defense, or sustainable energy—we must strive to harness our collective ingenuity in ways that promote peace and safeguard human dignity.

"The quest for innovation is eternal," reflects a modern strategist in a recent symposium. "But with each new technology, we must ask ourselves: What is the cost, and at what price are we willing to pay for progress? The legacy of our past teaches us that true strength lies not only in our machines but in our ability to learn, adapt, and, ultimately, to choose a path that honors both our potential and our humanity."
— Contemporary Military Theorist

A Legacy of Adaptation and Hope

In the interplay between steel and spirit, between cold technological precision and the warm pulse of human determination, lies the enduring legacy of World War II innovation. The breakthroughs of that era serve as a beacon—a reminder that even in the face of immense challenges, curiosity and the will to adapt can lead to profound transformations. They compel us to honor the sacrifices made, to learn from the ethical dilemmas encountered, and to channel our collective ingenuity toward a future where progress is measured not only in technological prowess but also in the betterment of humanity.

As we close this final chapter, let us reflect on the paradox of innovation: its power to both destroy and to rebuild, to instill fear and to inspire hope. In every modern military system, every advanced piece of technology, and every strategic decision, echoes the lessons of a time when the human drive to overcome adversity reshaped the very nature of warfare. May this legacy of curiosity and resilience continue to guide us, reminding us that in every challenge lies the potential for renewal and that the quest for progress is, at its heart, a journey toward a more thoughtful, just, and hopeful future.

Made in United States
Cleveland, OH
09 May 2025

16789671R00118